counseling
children
a
core issues
approach

Richard W. Halstead
Dale-Elizabeth Pehrsson
Jodi Ann Mullen

AMERICAN COUNSELING ASSOCIATION
5999 Stevenson Avenue • Alexandria, VA 22304
www.counseling.org

counseling children
a
core issues
approach

10   9   8   7   6   5   4   3   2

American Counseling Association
5999 Stevenson Avenue
Alexandria, VA 22304

Director of Publications   Carolyn C. Baker

Production Manager   Bonny E. Gaston

Editorial Assistant   Catherine A. Brumley

Copy Editor   Beth Ciha

Cover and text design by Bonny E. Gaston

Library of Congress Cataloging-in-Publication Data
Halstead, Richard W.
Counseling children: a core issues approach / Richard W. Halstead, Dale-Elizabeth Pehrsson, Jodi Mullen.
    p. cm.
  Includes bibliographical references and index.
  ISBN 978-1-55620-283-4 (alk. paper)
  1. Children—Counseling of   I. Pehrsson, Dale-Elizabeth.   II. Mullen, Jodi Ann.   III.   Title.
RJ504.H347 2011
618.92—dc22   2010038755

This book is dedicated to all children past and present.

• • •

table of contents

part I

A Working Orientation

part II

Intervention Modalities and Children's Core Issues

preface

For all children, life is a challenging endeavor. Many are constantly experiencing who they are; testing alternative ways to live their lives; and exploring opportunities for love, safety, and joy. Some children are forced to cope with overwhelming experiences, resulting in the loss of all of the best aspects of childhood. It is the counselor's role, of course, to assist children who may be experiencing a whole host of difficulties through no fault of their own. The purpose of this book is to enhance counselors' abilities to attend more completely to the core elements of problems children present.

Among the many complex factors involved in the counseling process, two are crucial: accurately conceptualizing the underlying nature of a child's struggle and designing an appropriate counseling plan to adequately address the problematic issues at hand. Often, counseling is made all the more difficult because of any number of limitations associated with early stages of physical, cognitive, and emotional development. Counselors who work with children will find this book to be a valuable tool for both expanding basic concepts of problem assessment and designing effective treatment modalities.

At their most basic level, children who present problems can be roughly grouped into two different categories (Halstead, 2007). In the first category are those who present problems resulting from some unexpected event or isolated situation. In these cases, the child usually presents with no remarkable problematic history. In the second category are those children who arrive with difficulties that are more complex in nature. Their issues reflect a larger set of significant patterns of problematic emotions and behaviors that have been in place for some longer period of time. Typically, a child in this second category presents problems that have a historical context and that therefore can be traced back to earlier points of that child's life and often to the nature of the relational environment in which the child lives. Thinking about these two broad categories can help a counselor establish a framework for understanding a bit better the nature of a child's presenting problem. It does little, however, to help the counselor design effective interventions. Even if the counselor can differentiate the type of presenting problem, without a means of framing what lies at the core of the problem he or she can become stuck and counseling interventions can meet with mixed results. With no framework for understanding the deeper nature of the child's problem—what we refer to in this book as the child's *core issues*—a counselor can often miss the bigger picture of the child's deeper struggle and the counseling process can falter and stall. The important goal of helping a child either adjust to a one-time situational event (the first category) or change repetitive problematic life patterns (the second category) is achieved more often by happenstance than by design. More important, the larger core issue(s) with which clients struggle but are unable to voice often remain unaddressed and thus are left unresolved, only to become the source of more serious problems in the future.

So we pose the following question: When a parent and child present for counseling, how does the counselor assess the nature of what is really happening at the core of the child's struggle? Although the answer will vary to some degree among counselors, it quickly becomes clear that well-schooled and talented counselors do not have a framework for understanding the core issues with which children struggle every day.

Limitations of the Widely Accepted Diagnostic Model: The *Diagnostic and Statistical Manual of Mental Disorders*

The problem of identifying and working effectively with core issues is not limited to less experienced clinicians. We have come to believe that the problem is more systemic in nature. As clinicians, we have on more than a few occasions been privy to information pertaining to children who have been hospitalized for inpatient treatment. These admissions are usually meant to assist the child through a severe crisis. It was after one such hospital case conference that the first author (Halstead) began to wonder about the power of models used for conceptualizing how a client presents. A constructivist would hold that conceptual models strongly influence what clinicians look for and, as a result, see in a child's presentation. In hospital settings, symptom classification according to the *Diagnostic and Statistical Manual of Mental Disorders* (4th ed., text rev.; *DSM–IV–TR*; American Psychiatric Association, 2000) is where client assessment and treatment planning starts and, all too often, ends. The American Psychiatric Association is currently working on the production of the *DSM–5*, which is due to be released in 2013. Given that the work committees have provided little advance information on the structure of this forthcoming work, it is unknown whether the *DSM–5* will move to a relational diagnostic focus. However, we are thinking that such a radical shift is highly unlikely.

The first *DSM* was published by the American Psychiatric Association in 1952. One might wonder how the mental health field might be different today if the counseling profession had spent the past 58 years engaged in an effort to develop a classification system for understanding the core nature of client problems. If such a system had been developed, would today's counselors focus their attention and interventions on qualitatively different aspects of a child's reported difficulties? Would there be greater support for relational or human growth and development–based models of diagnosis and intervention in the field of counseling? What if the counseling profession had developed a complete companion manual to the *DSM–IV–TR* (American Psychiatric Association, 2000) that focused on something other than sets of psychiatric symptoms as a means of conceptualizing the problems of childhood? What impact would a system that focused on relationally based core problematic issues have on a counselor's work? Imagine if, instead of only determining categories of disorders, the counseling profession offered clinicians a means of assessing the nature of children's core issues. Would having a framework that organized the basic thematic aspects of the relationally based difficulties children face help form better understandings of children's responses to difficult struggles in life? We propose that the answer to this question is an unqualified yes!

At this point it must be made clear that counselors should not ignore the fact that some individuals benefit greatly from medical model–based interventions. Furthermore, counselors must respect the fact that symptoms associated with current classifications of psychiatric disorders are synonymous with human suffering and, thus, they need to attend to intervention strategies that enhance the likelihood of symptom reduction. We are not suggesting that there is no place for medically based assessment and treatment as a primary or ancillary intervention in one's overall counseling practice. What we are suggesting is that, like any model, conceptualizations of client problems based on the *DSM–IV–TR* (American Psychiatric Association, 2000) have their limitations. We also argue that the counselor can move beyond these limitations by using alternative models for conceptualizing client problems.

One of the many major contributions that the multicultural counseling movement has made to the counseling profession involves advancing the notion that a wide variety of valid perspectives can be used for constructing a view of the world (Pedersen, 2001). Each variation carries with it a contextual basis for establishing an understanding of the nature of self, the social and relational roles of others, and a personal framing of the world's natural order. The result, from a social and cultural perspective, is the construction of qualitatively different belief systems that serve to inform lives. Each culture individually can only be understood from within its own unique and relativistic perspectives. It is through these ideas that members of the counseling profession have become sensitized to the idea that holding singularly absolute views of the world can limit and marginalize the validity of others. Culturally sensitive counselors have broader meaning-making frameworks for understanding that differences are often based in the unique dynamics of cultural social systems that orient an individual's worldview. This framing of culture and culturally based perspectives suggests that when the counselor has more than one model for understanding the nature of the world, it is possible to see and understand aspects of life that previously were invisible or incomprehensible. We contend that the very same principles apply to the diagnostic conceptualization and understanding of children's problems. Having only one formalized framework for diagnosing the nature of client problems is tantamount to imposing a culture of pathology on every child who is seen for counseling service. We are suggesting that this form of clinical encapsulation serves neither the child nor the counseling profession well.

A Different Conceptual Model

There is great merit in a problem classification framework that allows counselors to better understand the core elements of a child's struggle as opposed to limiting assessment to sets of observable symptoms. Having such a framework would not only enable counselors to better understand a child's presenting problems but also assist him or her in expressing these concerns. With such a framework, counselors would be able to address the core elements that serve to generate problematic responses and help the client discover and more effectively cope with the thematic threads that run through various problematic situations. These thematic threads could then come to serve as working reference points from which new and perhaps more adaptive personal perspectives could be generated. The motivation for advancing such an approach rests fully on the desire to bring resolution to the child's presenting concern and at the same time offer a means for helping the client create lasting change.

Having a framework that categorizes the nature of a client's core issues can enhance a counselor's work in four major ways. First, such a framework allows the counselor not only to conduct an accurate assessment of the client's stated concern but also to draw some preliminary hypotheses about the core elements that may underlie the child's struggle. Second, once identified, the child's core issue becomes a focal point for designing an effective counseling plan and choosing appropriate intervention modalities. Third, the counselor is better able to systematically monitor the client's progress in making transformational change over the course of the counseling process. Fourth, by committing a portion of the clinical focus to the client's core issue, the counselor helps facilitate the type of change that decreases the likelihood of relapse (Young, Beck, & Weinberger, 1994).

The underlying question associated with this position is, of course, what core issues are responsible for establishing and maintaining problematic thoughts, feelings, behavior, and associated meanings in a child's life? This book advances the notion that a nomenclature based on core issues is clinically richer and more useful than the classification of symptoms associated with psychiatric disorders. It is our contention that a different problem nomenclature can be used as a basis for forming a clearer understanding of the core nature or essence of a client's problem-based struggles as well as the accompanying symptoms. Using this different, more expansive understanding of diagnostic assessment, counselors can design intervention strategies to assist a child in making core changes that are more adaptive over the long term. One might think of the ideas presented in this book as important and valuable adjuncts to the use of the *DSM–IV–TR* (American Psychiatric Association, 2000). Put simply, we wrote this book to help the counselor formulate an understanding of the child client that is qualitatively different from that offered by the traditional psychiatric diagnosis and to demonstrate our model's applicability across treatment modalities. Our hope is that the utilization of this nomenclature will help the counselor understand the core elements of the child's presenting problem and use appropriate core issue–based interventions to help create lasting change.

This book draws heavily on the creative ingenuity of members of the counseling profession who have advanced theoretical perspectives in cognitive, play, art, and narrative therapies, all for the purpose of helping children live better quality lives. Most notably, we have drawn on the work of Jeffery Young, PhD, who built on earlier theoretical concepts to propose a cognitively oriented and relationally based diagnostic framework. Although these ideas are not fully ours, we believe that the real contribution of this book is in offering a unique integration and synthesis of theoretical perspectives that can enhance a counselor's work with children. Thus, we have made every effort to present the ideas and concepts in a concise manner that lends itself well to clear clinical application for the practicing counselor as well as the counseling student.

Overview of Book

The chapters in this book have been grouped into two parts. Part I contains four chapters that provide a basic orientation as to how counselors might think about the nature of clients' presenting problems. Chapter 1 sets the stage for considering alternatives to assessing a client's presenting problem(s) and the client's responses to his or her struggles. Chapter 2 offers a theoretical overview of the proposed diagnostic framework. This chapter briefly traces the conceptual framework of the core issues model and the validity of the construct. It also explains the 18 core issues that might be at work in a child's life and discusses the specific origin of each core issue. Chapter 3 provides a detailed framing of the thematic nature of core issues and how they are expressed as a living story detailed in a client's relational history and current stage of life. Chapter 4 extends the use of the child's living story as a narrative and acts as a conceptual bridge from the core issues assessment to effective intervention modalities. It also traces the counseling process through the use of a case study.

Part II addresses the elements involved in applying the core issues concept across widely accepted treatment modalities for working with children. Chapter 5 addresses the critical elements involved in establishing strong counseling relationships with children, the required sensitivities that pertain to certain developmental stages, and the nuance of entering into a child's world. Chapter 6 illustrates how, when cores issues themes emerge as narratives, the counselor can assist the child in giving voice to pain and struggle through a coconstructed story and how, through the reshaping of that story, the child can find a new way of being in the world. Chapter 7 discusses how counselors can address a core issue problem through the use of child-centered counseling and play therapy. Chapter 8 addresses sand work in counseling children and how this can be an effective modality for connecting with children's core issue themes and working through an identified problem. Chapter 9 provides an overview of the creative art approach to counseling and uses a case study to illustrate this form of intervention. Chapter 10 points out the important role that the counselor plays in helping to shape the efforts of parents, teachers, and other professionals in meeting a child's needs. This chapter makes it clear that helping a group of concerned adults to move in the same direction presents some formidable challenges. Each of these challenges is clearly delineated, and suggestions are offered as to how the counselor can work toward overcoming them.

acknowledgments

We would like to emphasize that this work has resulted from drawing on the creative works of many scholars, past and present, who have developed better methods for helping others and who have made the effort to publish their theoretical perspectives and research findings.

• • •

Richard W. Halstead would like to acknowledge the members of his family who value and foster a life of the mind. In addition, he acknowledges Ms. Stacy McHugh, whose diligent work as a graduate assistant helped to bring this project forward with much quality and clarity. He would like to extend heartfelt gratitude to Carolyn Baker, Director of Publications at the American Counseling Association, for all of the time and attention she has given to this project. Finally, a special thanks goes to Dr. Linda Wagner, who early on helped in key ways to stimulate thinking about the concept of core issues as an assessment framework.

• • •

Dale-Elizabeth Pehrsson would like to thank her husband, Dr. Robert S. Pehrsson, for his patience, laughter, and gift of time during this writing venture. She would also like to thank her students, clients, and family, who continue to inspire her and feed her spirit.

• • •

Jodi Ann Mullen would like to thank her coauthors Rick and Dale for being outstanding mentors and collaborators! Her husband Michael and children Andrew and Leah were amazingly supportive and were patient and understanding every time she said she needed to write. Finally, she thanks her running buddies, June, Sam, and Abby, who kept her moving forward on the running course as well as on the course of life.

about the authors

Richard W. Halstead, PhD, currently serves as professor and chair for the Department of Counseling and Family Therapy at Saint Joseph College in West Hartford, CT. He has published research articles in American Counseling Association journals on the nature of the counseling relationship and relationally based perspectives for engaging clients in processes of maturation and change. This focused work led to the writing of *Assessment of Client Core Issues* (2007). Dr. Halstead was chosen by students and faculty at Saint Joseph College to receive the John Stack Award for Excellence in Teaching.

● ● ●

Dale-Elizabeth Pehrsson, EdD, serves as associate dean of education and professor in the Department of Counselor Education at the University of Nevada, Las Vegas. Dr. Pehrsson has extensive experience working with children and families in clinical, school, and private practice settings as both a licensed professional counselor and a registered nurse. She is a Clinical Licensed Professional Counselor and Supervisor, Advanced (CLPC-S Idaho) and is certified by the National Board of Certified Counselors with specialization in supervision and distance counseling (National Certified Counselor, Approved Clinical Supervisor, Distance Credentialed Counselor). Furthermore, she is a registered play therapist and supervisor. She recently served as clinical editor for *Play Therapy Magazine*, the international publication of the Association for Play Therapy, as well as editor for the Association for Play Therapy Mining Online Series. Dr. Pehrsson is cofounder and clinical director of the Bibliotherapy Education Project. She serves as a peer reviewer on several editorial boards, including that of the *Journal for Creativity in Mental Health*.

● ● ●

Jodi Ann Mullen, PhD, LMHC, NCC, RPT-S, is an associate professor at the State University of New York at Oswego in the Counseling and Psychological Services Department, where she is the coordinator of the Graduate Certificate Program in Play Therapy and the Mental Health Counseling program. She is the Director of Integrative Counseling Services in Cicero and Oswego, New York. Dr. Mullen is a credentialed play therapist and play therapy supervisor. She is the author of several articles on play therapy and supervision. Her books include *Counseling Children and Adolescents Through Grief and Loss* (2006; coauthored with Dr. Jody Fiorini), *Play Therapy Basic Training: A Guide to Learning and Living the Child-Centered Play Therapy Philosophy* (2007), and *Supervision Can Be Playful: Techniques for Child and Play Therapist Supervisors* (2008; coedited with Athena Drewes). Dr. Mullen is on the editorial board of the *International Journal of Play Therapy*. She is also the Clinical Editor of *Play Therapy* magazine. Dr. Mullen was the 2008 recipient of the Professional Education and Training Key Award through the Association for Play Therapy.

● ● ●

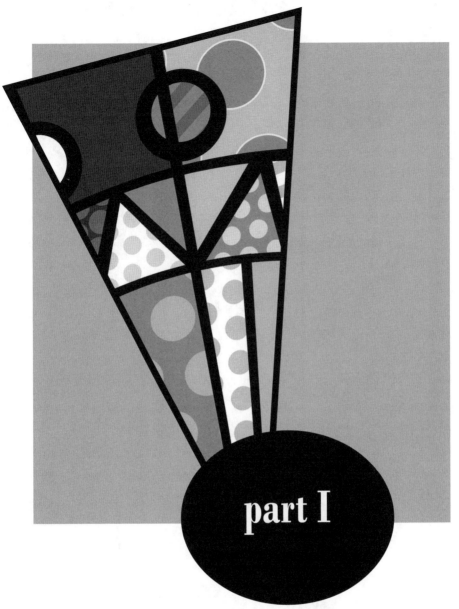

part I

A Working Orientation

an introduction
to children's core issues

Matthew is a 10-year-old African American boy who lives in a small suburban town. Matthew's family is considered middle class; his parents both have college educations. His father works at the nuclear power plant, and his mother is a school nurse. Matthew has younger twin siblings, Selina and Mikal, who are 5 years old. Matthew clearly states to most people who ask that he "hates" them. His parents are beside themselves as they describe Matthew's problem behaviors.

Matthew was referred for counseling services by his pediatrician. Over the past 2 years, he has become increasingly aggressive, oppositional, moody, and anxious. He refuses to go to school each morning and has gone as far as hiding the car keys (his parents drive him to school) and pouring tomato soup in the toilet in an attempt to trick his parents into believing that he has vomited. He cries every morning before school and begs his parents to home school him. He complains during the school day of stomach pain and dizziness. Matthew reports that he has no friends and that the teachers hate him. He goes to the school counselor almost daily because he doesn't want the other children in his class to see him cry.

• • •

Johnna is a 7-year-old Caucasian girl. She is in her second foster care home in 3 years. This home is supposed to be a preadoptive placement. Johnna's biological father is unknown, and her biological mother lost her parental rights after repeated charges of abuse and neglect. Johnna has three older siblings (ages 12, 16, and 18) who continue to live with their mother. Johnna is a friendly and spirited child. She is also irritable and full of rage, and her moods are unpredictable. She was removed from her previous foster care placement because she attempted to hurt younger children. At school she is disruptive in the classroom and is often removed to sit in the principal's office. As a result of these problems, she is lagging behind her peers academically. Yet Johnna is sure about one thing: She never wants to see her biological mom again. She emphatically states, "I hope she is dead! I want this lady [the new foster care parent] to be my new mommy."

• • •

These brief stories represent just some of the challenging problems children present when they enter counseling. The basic steps of the counseling process include forming a relationship with the child, accurately assessing the nature of the child's problem and related outcome goals, constructing a counseling plan, and implementing that plan in an attempt to bring about the desired results. The work that the counselor will do with a child in counseling is largely determined by the perspective used to define the problematic nature of the child's struggle.

This chapter addresses the current state of diagnosing childhood disorders and offers an expanded view of how alternative models for understanding children can enhance the assessment process. It provides a critical analysis of current standards for assessing the nature of children's problems and the ways in which a one-size-fits-all approach to clinical assessment may not be the most advantageous for counselors' work with children and their families.

A Critical Examination of the Clinical Diagnosis of Children

The current standard for arriving at a clinical diagnosis in the mental health professions is through the use of the clinical diagnostic interview. Typically, the counselor gathers information from the parents and the child and then matches that information with a system of diagnostic nomenclature. The system of nomenclature most widely used in the United States is the *Diagnostic and Statistical Manual of Mental Disorders* (4th ed., text rev.; *DSM–IV–TR*; American Psychiatric Association, 2000). This medically based system of assessment and diagnosis has been useful in giving practitioners and researchers a common language for the identification of psychiatric disorders. This system has also provided the clinician with three specific parameters for treatment. First, the *DSM* system sets criteria for determining whether a diagnostic threshold for a particular psychiatric disorder has been met. Second, the system provides the clinician with a set of target symptoms to be reduced or alleviated during treatment. Third, it provides a set of symptom-based benchmarks against which the clinician can monitor the client's functioning (Halstead, 2007).

In the past 20 years great strides have been made in establishing pharmaceutical and psychological treatment protocols aimed at controlling, reducing, or alleviating psychiatric symptoms as defined by the *DSM* system of nomenclature (Antony & Barlow, 2001; Levitt, Hoffman, Grisham, & Barlow, 2001). As helpful as the *DSM–IV–TR* is in providing a standard for diagnosing pathology and developing treatments, it has some inherent limitations in terms of addressing the issues presented by children (Callahan & Panichelli-Mindel, 1996). The American Psychiatric Association work committees are currently in the process of producing the next generation of diagnostic criteria for the *DSM–5*, which is expected to be published in 2013. Information addressing the production of the *DSM–5* has yet to appear in the literature, so we do not yet know what types of adaptations will be included to assess children's problems more holistically, but it seems unlikely that the diagnostic system as a whole will be revised to operate from a more broadly based relational perspective.

Unique Problems and Issues in Diagnosing Children With *DSM* Nomenclature

Using the *DSM* system to diagnose and treat children poses challenges similar to and different from the challenges encountered in using the *DSM* system in general. The limitations demonstrated in adult-centric diagnoses are also present in diagnoses of childhood disorders. However, diagnosis and treatment protocols are further complicated by the client's age and status as a member of the culture of childhood. In fact, L. Seligman (1998) argued that therapists who work with children must be specially skilled diagnosticians. Much of what is confusing about diagnosing children is linked to the *DSM* system of nomenclature itself. Children's mental health presentations are often confused by issues related to comorbidity and the plasticity of symptoms presented during the early stage of development, which is extremely dynamic (Sterba, Egger, & Angold, 2007; Todd, Huang, & Henderson, 2008).

The competent mental health professional must have knowledge of life-span development. Many of the behaviors that children display can be pathologized by parents even though they are typical for the child's stage of development. For example, one of us had a 3-year-old client referred to mental health counseling for "not listening and responding" to parental commands. Pathologizing the behaviors of children is often the product of a rush toward finding a diagnostic label for behavior. Most children display behaviors that are consistent with disorders listed in the *DSM*; however, the context, the child's age, and the rate of occurrence of any given behavior has to be viewed through a developmental lens if accurate assessment and treatment planning are to take place. The *DSM* system of nomenclature does not fully account for this complexity. Therefore, a working understanding of development is a necessary precursor to making accurate and thoughtful assessments, diagnoses, and treatment plans (M. Cameron & Guterman, 2007).

Children are also likely to come to therapy with an existing diagnosis provided by medical or academic professionals (L. Seligman, 1998). Because children (not unlike adults) can present very differently depending on the context, counselors working with children need to be comprehensive and thorough in their assessment. Missing the richness of a child's presentation would of course lead to poor treatment planning.

The contextual and relational aspects of children's lives are often minimized in the *DSM* system of nomenclature. The problems of children often seem obvious, however the way in which these problems are defined and subsequently treated are not. The fact that many factors contribute to the complexity of diagnosis makes the *DSM* system too simplistic. Ultimately, diagnosis (and therefore treatment) is influenced by conceptual models; purposes of definitions; the complexities of measuring emotions and behavior; definitions of normal and deviant behavior; relationships among social, academic, emotional, and behavioral disorders; development; and the limitations inherent in labeling itself (Kauffman, 2001).

Beach, Wamboldt, Kaslow, Heyman, and Reiss (2006) pointed out the correlation between individual mental health and the capacity for engaging in self-enhancing relational processes. This correlation is especially strong when one considers the clinical population of children. Children's process and progress in treatment are measured by stakeholders (e.g., parents and teachers) through relationships. Beach et al. suggested that given the importance that these relational processes play in an individual's healthy functioning, incorporating a relationally based assessment is a necessary part of rendering a diagnosis. Yet models for conducting relationally based assessment have fallen far behind in favor of a focus on psychiatric diagnostic nomenclature.

Using the DSM–IV–TR for Diagnosis

The basic elements necessary to reach a medically based diagnosis typically include the following: the type and frequency of symptoms associated with a particular syndrome; the duration of those symptoms; medical conditions, past and present, that may suggest an organic cause for a disorder; the type and intensity of life stressors present; and the level of impaired functioning at present and over the past year. When one considers the amount of information typically gathered about a child during a thorough intake process and compares it with that needed to render a medically based diagnosis, it becomes clear that a five-axis *DSM* diagnosis is extremely limited in scope. Many of the dimensions critical to understanding a child's current problems and any problematic history regarding the nature of the child's relationship environment are not taken fully into account. For instance, the *DSM–IV–TR* attends only tangentially to the relational elements relevant to a child's life in the "V" codes (e.g., sibling relational problem, parent and child relational problem). Also found in the *DSM–IV–TR* is a listing of common psychosocial problems that are recorded on Axis IV (e.g., problems with primary support group, problems related to social environment). Axis V notations complete the diagnosis via scaled assessment for Global Assessment of Functioning and Global Assessment of Relational Functioning (see Appendix B of the *DSM–IV–TR*). Detailed aspects of a client's family history, perceptions of self over time, spiritual beliefs, and meaning attached to life events are extremely rich inputs for constructing an understanding of the nature of the person and not just the disorder. For the counselor who wishes to emphasize the nature of a client's experiential world and how it may relate to the client's problem, the nomenclature system embodied in the *DSM–IV–TR* falls short.

In addition, information gathered about children in treatment is rarely gathered from the children themselves but from parents, caregivers, or teachers (Mullen, 2003). Data from parents are likely to be biased, as many parents feel responsible for having to seek mental health services for their child and therefore present information from a position of guilt, shame, and defensiveness. Moreover, many clinicians have limited professional preparation in working clinically with children (Mullen, 2003) and therefore do not have the assessment skills needed to address the unique developmental and cultural aspects this population presents.

Whether a client's symptoms meet the diagnostic criteria for a particular disorder, or the client reports some symptoms but not enough to meet the diagnostic threshold for a disorder, or the client presents a problem broad in nature that would normally be classified as a *DSM–IV–TR* V-code problem, the medically based system does not always serve counselors well (Kaslow, 1996; Kihlstrom, 2002). Put simply, a medically based system of nomenclature that emphasizes pathology does not provide the counselor with a systematic means for conceptualizing the core nature of a client's struggle. Knowing whether a child is depressed or anxious does not aid the counselor in developing a deeper understanding of the core issues that may be the source of a client's diagnostic symptoms.

A major problem that professional counselors face daily is that the mental health industry has been built around the accurate classification of symptoms, whereas assessment of the core nature of a child's problem is often left to unstructured conjecture. Yet counselors who seek to use the theoretical concepts of human growth and development and who want to focus on the core issues central to a child's difficulty would be ill advised to do this without also incorporating a medical model perspective. First, some psychiatric disorders are tied to organic abnormalities and need to be treated medically. Second, an accurate assessment of the nature of any pathology a child may exhibit is valuable because it provides important reference points for gathering further information, establishing counseling goals, and constructing a counseling plan. Third, failure to establish a *DSM–IV–TR* assessment as a diagnostic reference point would surely raise questions about whether the counselor was fulfilling an ethical and legal responsibility to meet the standard of care established by the mental health profession (Corey, Corey, & Callanan, 2007; Madden, 1998). Fourth, any counselor who relies on a third-party payer for the payment of fees must select a *DSM–IV–TR* diagnosis code. Therefore, even though the psychiatric nomenclature may not fit well with health, wellness, relational, or developmental frames of reference, counselors often must use it as a standard for the delivery of counseling services.

Limitations of the *DSM–IV–TR* Assessment Model

Burke (1989) suggested that there is a basic dichotomy in working orientations for clinical intervention based on client need: (a) stabilization and reduction of the child's symptoms and (b) the child's acquisition of a new or more finely developed coping skill repertoire resulting from engaging in the counseling process. As one might surmise, each of these working orientations is associated with qualitatively different outcome goals. The first category, stabilization and reduction of symptoms, is commonly associated with medically oriented models that conceptualize clients as struggling with pathological syndromes. The central questions asked in a medically based treatment orientation are as follows:

- What are the symptoms related to any particular diagnostic syndrome?
- What has been the duration of these symptoms?
- How can the symptoms be reduced to premorbid levels?

The following case example serves well to illustrate these elements.

Gregory's parents are concerned about him. They have discussed with Gregory's pediatrician the possibility of a psychopharmacological intervention for what they describe as anxiety. Over the past year, Gregory has developed "tics" in his legs. Sometimes when he is walking he loses control because of these tics and falls down. He also incessantly wrings his hands. Within the past 4 months he has begun soiling and wetting himself. His father indicates that Gregory is oblivious to these accidents. Finally, Gregory has been having trouble falling and staying asleep. This is very troublesome to his parents, because he is now sleeping in their room. Gregory's pediatrician has ruled out a medical or physical etiology for Gregory's symptoms.

Applying the stabilization orientation to working with a child such as Gregory, the counselor knows that the child is anxious, that the symptoms have been present for 4 to 12 months, and that the child's anxiety has a particular level of severity. Once the diagnosis has been made, the counselor has a specific set of symptom markers against which progress can be tracked over the course of counseling. Because some disorders correlate positively with certain risk concerns, the counselor must always be certain to assess and continually monitor the nature and severity of the symptoms that the child presents. In the case of an older child diagnosed with severe depression, for example, a counselor would surely want to make every effort to assess for suicidal ideation and recent actions that may suggest the client is at risk for engaging in harmful behavior.

However, a close examination of the client stabilization or symptom reduction orientation reveals some limitations to its usefulness. The first limitation is that not every child who is experiencing problems that warrant attention meets the criteria for a psychiatric disorder. In such cases, the professional counselor is often left with no alternative nomenclature structure to systematically conceptualize the true nature of the child's problem(s). The counselor who continues to think in terms of DSM–IV–TR diagnostic categories has two choices. First is the "close enough" approach. Even though the child's symptoms do not meet all of the criteria for a particular disorder, the counselor can use the symptoms that are present to point in the direction of a specific diagnosis. In those situations, the counselor might use phrases such as "the child exhibits depressive-like presentation" or "the child shows some evidence of an anxiety disorder." The second choice is to look at the broader problem being presented and use the section of the *DSM–IV–TR* labeled "Other Conditions That May Be a Focus of Clinical Attention," commonly referred to as the "V codes." Categories such as relationship problem not otherwise specified, academic problem, or parent–child relational problem are so broad that they offer little help in arriving at a specific conceptualization of the problem, let alone specific interventions to include in a counseling plan.

The second limitation of the *DSM–IV–TR* system is that it can be adopted as a generalized view of the world. That is, the counselor begins to perceive a world in which pathology abounds and understands that every child presents with some form of pathology. When one is formally trained and experienced in the use of a classification system oriented toward the assessment and diagnosis of pathology, it is only reasonable to expect that pathology is indeed what one will recognize, assess, and ultimately diagnose. Put most simply, one cannot name that which one does not know. With no juxtaposing lens through which to view a child's problematic struggle, a clinician can fall into the habit of pathologizing even normative responses to troubling events in the child's life. This is a special concern when framing pathology across cultures (Comas-Diaz, 1996): The variation in normative response must be understood relative to the child's worldview and the context of culturally normative patterns and rituals. Broad definitions of culture include age as a variable (Pedersen & Ivey, 1993). Therefore, childhood itself can be defined as a unique culture and must be taken into consideration in the overall assessment process.

The third limitation of this working orientation pertains to the treatment objectives associated with a stabilization and symptom reduction treatment frame. Although stabilization and symptom reduction is an important first phase of counseling, limiting outcome goals to reducing the symptoms associated with a particular disorder can result in missed opportunities to help foster the child's growth and development.

An Alternative Diagnostic Framework

The second category of Burke's (1989) dichotomy of interventions is oriented toward client growth and maturation. The life-span development perspective has a very long history in the field of counseling and serves as a hallmark for the profession (Barnes, 2003). By fostering growth around a presenting problem or issue, the client will learn how to deal with similar problematic life issues differently, thereby reducing the likelihood of a relapse (Young et al., 1994). The counselor choosing to work from a model that emphasizes human development must ask and answer a set of questions that are qualitatively different from those associated with a medically based treatment model. Whereas the medical model poses questions about the nature of the client's disorder, a growth-oriented model addresses a very different type of clinical challenge.

Growth-oriented questions focus on the nature of the child's perceptual world and resulting problematic relational patterns. For example, a counselor working with Matthew (described at the opening of this chapter) from a growth-oriented perspective would pose questions such as the following: What relational factors are at play that would cause Matthew to report that he hates his younger sisters? What is it that Matthew is resisting with his oppositional behavior? What threat is Matthew perceiving that would account for his level of anxiety? What experiences might he be avoiding by hiding his parents' car keys and staging illness? By investigating questions such as these, the counselor begins to address different dimensions of "the problem." Growth and development questions reveal aspects of the child's life that may not be congruent with longer term prosocial goals and that may reflect a pattern that serves to keep the problem in place. In Matthew's case, such questions can help to develop a better understanding of his relational worldview and can reveal the elements that are at the core of his recurrent problems in school and at home.

Posing client growth and maturation questions is not new. In some settings, these kinds of questions are quite common and often are part of a thorough psychosocial intake. It is unusual, however, for such questions and the information they generate to be used in a systematic manner as part of an integrated and structured diagnostic framework aimed specifically at assisting the clinician in forming a deeper understanding of a client's struggle. As Maslow (1971) warned, "If the only tool you have is a hammer, you tend to see every problem as a nail" (p. 56). It is time to seriously consider the manner in which members of the helping professions have been hammering away at clients' presenting issues via the classification of symptoms associated with frames of pathology. As M. E. Seligman and Csikszentmihalyi (2000) stated, "Treatment is not just fixing what is broken; it is nurturing what is best" (p. 7). To accomplish the goal of nurturing what is best, counselors need a structural framework with which to assess the nature of children's problems and a system of nomenclature that will help in accurately conceptualizing that with which the child struggles (Carruthers, Hood, & Parr, 2005).

Relationally based diagnostic frameworks such as the one first proposed by Young (1990) and subsequently refined have produced a system of problem nomenclature that is widely applicable to the counseling profession (Young, Klosko, & Weishaar, 2003). Our overall aim in presenting the current model is to help counselors develop an understanding of what client core issues are, how they originate, and the role that a core issues perspective can play in helping to design and implement effective counseling strategies that result in lasting change.

This approach to counseling requires that counselors and clients engage in a process of personal discovery and, ultimately, growth. The clinical dimensions of this work include establishing a trusting relationship, becoming clear about the client's personal history, exploring the client's current and past relationship experiences, finding meaning in the client's responses to problems, and creating a vision for the client's future. This work also involves a specific process of first identifying and then exploring the elements of an individual's life that impede goal-congruent activities and how the counselor can intervene in a manner that supports the client in achieving lasting change (Tursi & Cochran, 2006).

Summary

As the field of counseling has broadened in recent decades to meet society's mental health needs, there has been a steady move to conceptualize the nature of client problems with models that promote the diagnosis of pathology. The alignment of the counseling profession with psychiatry and clinical psychology has, in some ways, been a necessity, as interdisciplinary treatment, managed care, and case law have all shaped the current standard of care that counselors must meet. Unfortunately, this alignment has limited how counselors assess problems and design interventions to address children's core issues.

conceptual foundations for understanding client core issues

In Chapter 1 we argued for the adoption of a complimentary diagnostic nomenclature for assessing the core nature of issues with which children struggle. This chapter provides an overview of how core issues originate under psychosocial stress and how they are conceptualized. It also offers descriptive definitions for each of the 18 core issue categories that compose the model.

Origin of Client Core Issues and Emotion-Focused Coping

According to Herman (1992), over the last half of the 20th century increased attention was given to the impact of acute traumatic events. The severe impact of acute traumatic events is a well-established source of serious psychological and emotional problems (Chu, 1992). However, it is also important to recognize the serious impact of persistent negative events that fail to meet the threshold of acute trauma but yet have a profound effect on children when experienced over extended periods of time. Young et al. (1994) suggested that exposure to such events can create a host of difficult problems. Repeated losses, betrayals, bullying, or growing up under excessively rigid standards are just a few examples of the types of relational experiences that can have a profound impact on a child's emotional world and therefore can become a source of psychological and emotional problems (Muldoon, 2003).

A negative problematic event may occur for one of many different reasons during one's formative years and result in emotional wounds that can last long after the experience itself has passed (Halstead, 1996, 2007; Schneiders et al., 2006). Such wounding is a special concern with children who lack the power and skill repertoire to effectively change the environment in which they live. Children who can neither change a negative situation nor remove themselves from that environment must find a means of coping with the noxious elements in their environment. According to Lazarus (1991), "Coping consists of cognitive and behavioral efforts to manage specific external or internal demands that are appraised as taxing or exceeding the resources of the person" (p. 112). Figure 1 depicts a simplified graphic representation of a coping process that was first proposed by Lazarus and Folkman (1984) and then elaborated further by Lazarus. The model holds that a person possesses sets of goal commitments, beliefs, individual preferences, temperament, character, and a base of knowledge that come together to form a basic psychological structure. Each of these component elements is used to assess the nature of situational conditions experienced at any moment in time. Presented with a situation from the environment, the person will first respond by conducting what Lazarus and Folkman referred to as a *primary appraisal*. That is, he or she will analyze the nature of the environmental stimulus and determine whether it is consistent or inconsistent with personally formed goal commitments, beliefs, and knowledge. In this way, the person is construing the basic nature of the situation and the degree to which it is a threat. The main question associated with this primary appraisal is "What is the nature of this situation, and is it a threat to either me or the goals to which I am committed?"

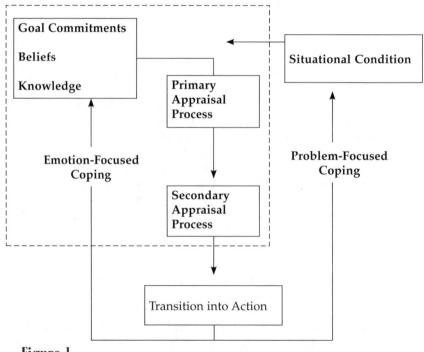

Figure 1
Stressor Threat Model of Coping

If the situational condition is indeed assessed as a threat, the individual will move to the next step in the coping process, which is to engage in what Lazarus and Folkman (1984) referred to as a *secondary appraisal*. This personal inventorying of skills, abilities, and social support resources involves assessing the resources one possesses to deal with the situational condition. The process also involves the individual assessing his or her specific action tendencies, emotive affect, and physiological responses. These elements come together to determine the form of the specific coping action in which the individual will engage. Compared to adults, children generally have less power and more limited skills in their repertoires. The result is that they often have few options in the secondary appraisal phase of coping and thus are more vulnerable to stressful situational conditions.

There are two different forms of coping behavior: problem-focused and emotion-focused coping (Lazarus, 1991; Lazarus & Folkman, 1984). Both have the goal of minimizing distress associated with a problematic situational condition from the environment. As depicted in Figure 1, problem-focused coping is directed outward, with the goal of making some change to the situational condition in the environment. This form of coping is aimed at reducing negative experiences caused by the situational condition. One will usually only engage in problem-focused coping if, as a result of the secondary appraisal, it is believed that personal resources can be applied to change or reduce the stressful impact of the situational condition. If successful, problem-focused coping will modify or alleviate the stressful or threatening nature of the situational condition that is understood to be a threat to either one's self or one's goal commitments.

For example, Harry, an 8-year-old boy, helps his older brother Todd on his new early morning newspaper route in their neighborhood. There is one house on the route whose owners have let the shrubs become so overgrown that they create a very dark cave-like entryway up to the porch where the newspapers need to be placed. Harry is especially frightened to approach this house, given its dark and foreboding feel, especially as autumn months bring darker and darker mornings. Harry's first attempt at problem-focused coping is to get Todd to deliver papers to "the dark house" so that he will not have to be exposed to the perceived dangers associated with the house. Being a typical big brother, Todd refuses and tells Harry that he has to deliver to the house because it is on "his side of the street." Harry is beside himself as to what he can do to resolve this problem. As he continues to assess this situation and what he can do to better manage it, a solution comes to him. He remembers the camping headlamp that he received for his birthday, and in an instant he knows that his problem has been solved. Each morning from that point forward Harry throws on his headlamp, and when he comes to that dark house he switches on his light to illuminate the way, thereby removing the threat of the unknown.

In some cases, efforts to address and change the impact of the situational condition directly, as Harry did, can fail to bring about the desired result of reducing or alleviating the stressor. As a result of engaging in a secondary appraisal, a child may determine that he or she lacks the resources needed to successfully deal with the situational condition. In these instances, the child has no other choice but to respond by initiating emotion-focused coping strategies. Rather than focusing on changing or alleviating the situational condition, emotion-focused coping efforts rely primarily on various psychological processes to manage the negative effects that the stressor is having on the individual. Lazarus (1991) made the point that emotion-focused coping is a psychologically active process as opposed to one that is passive in nature. Emotion-focused coping involves the mobilization of internal activities in an attempt to minimize the effects of an unpleasant or threatening situational condition. According to Carver, Scheier, and Weintraub (1989), people can use a number of emotion-focused coping strategies, including planning, positive reinterpretation, and humor, to deal more effectively with many life stressors. Yet some strategies are less positive, including mental or emotional disengagement, behavioral disengagement, denial, the inappropriate venting of emotion, and a focus on negative emotional reactions.

As Figure 1 indicates, regardless of whether a child uses positive or negative emotion-focused coping strategies, this form of coping requires the child to make internal psychological and emotional adjustments. Emotion-focused coping necessitates some degree of modification to the child's goal commitments, beliefs, and knowledge. When the stressful situational condition is relational in nature and pertains to important emotional needs, the modifications the child makes will have a direct impact on the perceptions he or she has constructed about the self, others, and the world. In the next section, we discuss in greater detail the construction of the child's perceptual worldview as it relates to his or her emotional needs.

The Role of Core Emotional Needs

Core issues form between infancy and adolescence and result from emotional needs that have not been adequately met. Consider for a moment the most basic emotional needs that children strive to meet during childhood. A number of theoretical models have described the nature and importance of emotional needs during one's formative years. Erikson (1963) proposed a useful framework for examining core needs presented within eight psychosocial developmental stages. Erikson proposed that of those eight stages, the first five address the basic needs of a child developing from birth through adolescence (see Table 1). Erickson held that if a child's caregivers foster the child's development in a positive manner, the child will progress through the stages of psychosocial development in good stead. However, if the child's psychosocial environment does not support his or her basic needs, the child will experience difficulties (Erikson, 1963).

Staub (1999) discussed the nature of human behavior under conditions in which the fulfillment of basic human needs is frustrated:

Table 1
Erickson's (1963) Developmental Stages and Related Basic Needs

Age	Stage	Basic Needs
Birth–1½ years	Trust vs. Mistrust	Safety and security
1½–3 years	Autonomy vs. Doubt	Confidence and freedom from critical review
3–6 years	Initiative vs. Guilt	Freedom to express in play
6–11 years	Industry vs. Inferiority	Sense of competence
Adolescence	Identity vs. Role Confusion	Definition of self

We human beings have certain shared psychological needs that must be fulfilled if we are to lead reasonably satisfying lives: We need to feel secure; we need a positive identity; we need to feel effective and to have reasonable control over what is essential to us; we need both deep connections to other people and autonomy or independence; we need to understand the world and our place in it. (p. 183)

From a cognitive schema perspective, Young et al. (2003), drawing from theory and clinical research, offered a set of five core emotional needs that closely parallel those associated with Erikson's and Staub's perspectives. They proposed that the psychologically healthy individual can adapt to the environment in a manner such that he or she is able to meet each one of the five core emotional needs with some degree of adequacy. Table 2 lists the five core emotional needs and the nature of a relational environment that would support having those needs met, as proposed by Young et al. (2003).

It is clear from Table 2 that there is a direct connection between one's basic core needs and the relational environment to which one is exposed. This connection establishes the relational nature of the core issues with which many clients struggle.

Tied closely to core emotional needs are beliefs about the relational environment in which those needs are met and the influence these beliefs have on the child. Everly and Lating (2004) proposed a set of five broad

Table 2
Core Emotional Needs and the Required Relational Environments to Support Them

Core Emotional Need	Relational Environment
Secure attachment	Safe, stable, nurturing, and accepting
Autonomy, competence, identity	Action is initiated without excessive critical review
Expression of needs and emotions	Needs and emotions are respected and validated
Spontaneity of play	Expression of thought, feelings, and behavior
Realistic limits and self-control	Personal limits and boundaries are respected

core beliefs that frame the nature of human character and constitute "an essential thread within the fabric of human personality" (p. 33). These core psychological beliefs are (a) the importance of living in a fair and just world, (b) the importance of attaching to and trusting in other persons, (c) the importance of a physically safe environment, (d) the importance of a positive identity (e.g., esteem and efficacy), and (e) the belief in some overarching order to life (e.g., religion, spirituality, a defining order, a unifying paradigm).

The consistency and similarity of thought in the aforementioned perspectives pertaining to the core elements of basic emotional needs are striking (Erikson, 1963; Everly & Lating, 2004; Staub, 1999; Young et al., 2003). Taking these core needs into account, one could, with good reason, conclude that there must be a favorable psychosocial environment associated with becoming a well-adjusted individual. Put simply, children have core emotional and psychosocial needs that should be adequately met. Furthermore, the degree to which these core emotional needs are met depends largely on the quality of relational interactions within the environment. Relational encounters establish the sets of beliefs children hold about their personal worlds, and these sets of beliefs form the basis for determining the nature of future relational interactions (Langdridge, 2005).

Core Emotional Needs and Culture

When framing core emotional needs, one must question the universality of the concept. It is important to fully take into account the differences in how various cultures express such needs. One should exercise extreme caution in universally applying any one conceptual understanding across cultures or even across all individuals within any one culture. Counselors need to consider the degree to which any model used to formulate the nature of a child's problem may be culturally biased and how it may support one particular worldview over another (Ibrahim, Roysircar-Sodowsky, & Ohnishi, 2001). This determination is important in that it will dictate the degree to which any form of knowing can be applicable in guiding work with children and families whose worldviews may differ as a result of cultural affiliation (Erickson, 2002). Reaching a conclusion regarding the etic or emic nature of any perspective can, however, be difficult and requires the counselor to consider a variety of factors (e.g., the need for attachment presented in the aforementioned models of core emotional needs; Sue & Sue, 2003). For example, Grossmann, Grossmann, and Keppler (2005) clearly indicated that attachment need is a universal phenomenon among human infants. However, the method and means of fulfilling this need vary widely across cultures (Greenfield, Keller, Fuligni, & Maynard, 2003).

If one accepts the idea that humans share common emotional and psychological needs, the challenge then becomes considering how the expression of those needs is first articulated and then met in different cultures. The counselor must seek to understand how core needs are expressed and fulfilled within the child's cultural framework. In doing so, the counselor may find a broader multicultural applicability of core emotional needs as a basis for understanding.

More controversial are core emotional needs that are thought to come into play later in a child's development. Issues such as establishing autonomy and forming a personal identity have also been conceptualized as basic core emotional needs (Erikson, 1963; Everly & Lating, 2004; Staub, 1999; Young et al., 2003). It has been very well documented that culturally based differences exist in terms of the degree of individualism or collectivism within specific societies (Pedersen, 2001). Developing a degree of autonomy in establishing one's identity is a developmental task most closely associated with societies that reflect Western Euro-American cultural perspectives. If one examines how autonomy is defined by Young et al. (2003) in terms of a core emotional need (see Table 2), it should be clear that autonomy does not necessarily suggest an independent individualistic expression of self. Rather, their definition provides an option for considering a wide array of actions that are free from excessive criticism. That is, initiating autonomous action as a means of supporting or advancing the wishes of the collective group is just as valid as more individualistic expressions of autonomy. Focusing attention on how these concepts are expressed within different cultures allows for a broader applicability of the model. Doing so also decreases the likelihood of the counselor imposing culturally biased presuppositions that result in a narrow understanding of either the client or the foundation for the child's worldview, from which the meaning of self, others, and the nature of the world are constructed.

Cognitive Schemas and One's Relational Worldview

In order to understand the core issues framework and how it can serve as a reference point for addressing children's problems, counselors must become familiar with the basic principles and constructs upon which this perspective is based. The primary construct one must understand is that of cognitive schemas. Those already familiar with cognitive theories of counseling may have encountered this construct and its implications for clinical assessment and intervention design. For those who are not as well versed in cognitive models of counseling and therapy, we present here a brief introduction to the construct.

According to Young et al. (2003), the concept of schemas has been used by a variety of disciplines to convey the idea of a specific organizational structural theme or a framework. In the field of cognitive psychology, the term *schema* conveys the concept of an information-organizing structure used to establish meaning. For instance, Piaget (1969) discussed cognitive schemas as the primary cognitive structures that determine how children process information differently as they progress through specific stages of cognitive development. This use of the schema construct in cognitive psychology sets the stage for its application in cognitive therapy. In one of his earliest writings describing cognitive therapy and its application for the treatment of depression, Beck (1967) defined *schema* as a primary element that serves to frame one's perceptual reality:

> A schema is a structure for screening, coding, and evaluating the stimuli that impinge on the organism. It is the mode by which the environment is broken down and organized into its many psychologically relevant facets. On the basis of that matrix of schemata, the individual is able to orient himself [or herself] in relation to time and space and to categorize and interpret experiences in a meaningful way. (p. 283)

The essence of Beck's definition of a cognitive schema provides a means for conceptualizing the interaction between a child's active information processing and the environment. Wadsworth (1971) suggested that an organized set of schemas serves two functions. First, similar to Beck's formulation, schemas provide a primary means for processing information related to an experience and thereby establishing the meaning of that experience. Second, cognitive schemas provide the basis for formulating a response to the meaning that has been made from that experience.

It is interesting that the early works that popularized various forms of cognitive and cognitive–behavioral approaches to counseling and therapy did not focus on such concepts as basic schema structure or schema-based information processing models of therapy. Rather, those early works focused on ideas such as activating events, beliefs, automatic thoughts, internal dialogue, negative self-talk messages, and maladaptive assumptions (Beck, Rush, Shaw, & Emery, 1979; Beck & Young, 1985). According to Goldfried (2003), early cognitive-based interventions fell short of capturing the full picture of an individual's primary functioning and therefore generated interventions that were limited in scope and effectiveness. Furthermore, Goldfried held that it was not until cognitive therapy moved away from focusing solely on secondary elements of client functioning (e.g., self-statements) and began focusing on the primary elements of meaning-making structures (i.e., cognitive schemas) consistent with cognitive science that richer forms of therapeutic approaches advanced (Riso, du Toit, Stein, & Young, 2007).

As the essential organizers of meaning, cognitive schemas provide the conceptual framework for understanding how an individual establishes a worldview. Beck and Weishaar (1989) hypothesized that schemas are developed during childhood and become increasingly elaborate as one gains life experience. Applying the concept of schemas as defined by Beck (1967) to an individual's relational world, one can begin to consider a specific subset of relationally focused schemas established throughout childhood and adolescence that filter and evaluate the nature of relationship encounters. This subset of relationally based schemas is often referred to in the cognitive therapy literature as *early maladaptive schemas*. These maladaptive relational schemas are the source of difficulties as an individual interacts with the world and therefore are a first-order problem (Young et al., 2003). In fact, one can think of core issues as being the result of an individual establishing maladaptive relational schemas (Young, 1990), which generate the symptoms associated with many nonorganically based *DSM–IV–TR,* Axis I diagnoses and character disorders diagnosed on Axis II.

Early Maladaptive Schemas and Core Issues

Schemas can be classified as either positive or negative. Positive schemas organize meaning about the self, others, and the world in a variety of ways that are adaptive, whereas negative schemas organize meaning in a manner that is maladaptive in one's current environment (Sharf, 2004).

Young (1990, 1999) advanced the idea that repeated negative, toxic, or goal-incongruent experiences associated with trying to meet core emotional needs will form a special set of relationally based maladaptive schemas. Because these negative experiences are formed within the context of relational interactions, the schemas established around those relationships tend to skew an individual's relational worldview. When one forms maladaptive relational schemas, there is a resulting tendency to interact with others in a manner that impedes more adaptive functioning (Crawford & Wright, 2007). A key point related to this idea was posed by Freeman (1993), who suggested that the formation of negative schema-based response tendencies is adaptive when core emotional needs are not being met at a time when the child is powerless to change the relational environment. If the child carries these negative schema-based response tendencies into more normative venues, this can be broadly problematic. In essence, one can conceptualize problems as arising from the triggering of negative schemas that in turn leads to cognitive, affective, and behavioral responses that tend toward being self-defeating. In this sense, behavior that was once adaptive in one relational environment is understood to be maladaptive in a more normative relational environment. Over time, these self-defeating tendencies can become more generalized patterns of interaction that directly interfere with an individual's ability to fulfill specific needs, wants, and desires (Young, 1990, 1999). Because these maladaptive schemas are usually established during childhood, Young (1990) used the phrase *early maladaptive schemas* to describe them. He proposed that early maladaptive schemas have a particular set of descriptive characteristics that can be used to assess the core elements that are supporting problematic interactions in life. Given that these maladaptive schemas are usually formed in childhood, it would hold that they would serve as a useful framework for working with children.

According to Young et al. (2003), the most recent formulation of early maladaptive schemas consists of four broad descriptive elements. First, as previously stated, early maladaptive schemas usually develop as a direct result of one or more core emotional needs not being met on a consistent basis either in childhood or through adolescence. Second, without intervention or some other corrective set of emotional experiences, early maladaptive schemas are further refined and incorporated as part of the individual's relational worldview as that person moves through life. Third, early maladaptive schemas suggest specific relationally oriented themes or patterns that tend to be pervasive and as such can be traced over an individual's history. Fourth, when fully activated, these schemas generate an associated set of intense cognitions, emotions, and behavioral responses that interfere with meeting one's short-term and longer term goals. For that reason, early maladaptive schemas are thought of as being dysfunctional (Theiler & Bates, 2007).

Young's (1990, 1999) earliest formulations of early maladaptive schemas were as the basic core issues related to personality disorders. Young proposed that this subset of relational schemas could be used for both assessing the nature of particular personality disorders and designing more effective treatment for clients. In response to additional research and clinical application of this framework, the utility of early maladaptive schemas has been expanded to include not only personality disorders but also less severe character-related problems and Axis I psychiatric disorders (Ball, Mitchell, & Malhi, 2003; Cecero & Young, 2001; Flanagan, 1993; Hoffart, Versland, & Sexton, 2002; Lee, Taylor, & Dunn, 1999; Morrison, 2000; Schmidt, Joiner, Young, & Telch, 1995; Young & Flanagan, 1998; Young & Gluhoski, 1997; Young & Mattila, 2002; Young et al., 2003). This expansion in clinical application provides a valuable adjunct for those counselors looking to conceptualize the core nature of problems generally and, as we propose here, the problems experienced and expressed by children specifically. Assessing early maladaptive schemas provides a structured approach for arriving at the core issues that serve as the root cause of a child's distress. In addition, this form of assessment provides a counselor with a means for extending problem conceptualization beyond a process of symptom classification and fosters interventions that support client growth as well as symptom reduction.

Core Issues Defined

Core issues are an artifact of having developed one or more early maladaptive schemas. They are defined as the primary problematic elements of an individual's intrapersonal and interpersonal meaning-making system that, when activated, generate problematic responses to situational conditions over time.

To more fully grasp the concept of core issues, it is helpful to examine each portion of the definition separately. The first element in the definition of core issues addresses a client's intrapersonal and interpersonal experience. The importance of this focus rests on an underlying contention that all problems clients present are, in one form or another, relationship problems (Carnevale, 1989). Think for a moment about the relational nature of an individual's life. It can be argued that an individual is constantly engaged in relationship. The form of relationship one engages in is dictated by qualitatively different relational dyads. These dyads include the individual in relationship with self, with another or a group, and with the natural world. From a core issues perspective, these three formulations of relational connection constitute a relational triad. Thinking about the nature of relationships allows the counselor to better analyze those aspects of the problem with which the client is struggling and the intrapersonal or interpersonal dynamics of that struggle. Figure 2 shows the interactional aspects of the relational triad.

The relational triad allows the counselor to classify three different basic problem situations, all of which reflect a relational core issues perspective. These three basic relationally based problems follow the points contained in the relational triad: relational problem with self, with others, and with nature or the world (Burke, 1989; Carnevale, 1989). Figure 3 depicts this most basic nature of client problems.

The first two forms of relational problems are fairly straightforward. Relationship with self problems exist somewhere along the continuum "I hate myself" and "I love myself to the exclusion of others." The further one moves toward either end of the continuum, the more difficult one's experience will usually be. Relationship with other problems exist along the continuum "I am not getting what I want or need from others" (e.g., emotional support, empathy, love) and "I am getting what I do not want or need from others" (e.g., physical mistreatment, verbal abuse, emotional abuse, overprotection, smothering). Relationship with the world problems exist along the continuum "I am not getting what I want or need from the world" (e.g., goal-congruent events) and "I am getting what I do not want or need from the world" (e.g., goal-incongruent events).

Unlike the first two types of relationally oriented problems, the third type is less commonly addressed in the literature and perhaps is best explained through the use of an example. Imagine a young boy who has been diagnosed with cancer. His immediate response might be how unfair it is for him to have to deal with this disease, and he may move into an emotional response such as intense anger. In this situation, anger is rarely directed at the self or any individual in the child's life but rather at the seemingly cruel nature of how the world works at times. This example shows that one's relationship to the randomness of natural occurrences in life can become the source of a problem to which an individual will then

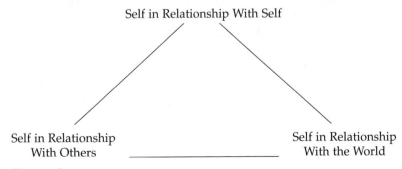

Self in Relationship With Self

Self in Relationship
With Others

Self in Relationship
With the World

Figure 2

Elements of the Relational Triad

Self with Self:	Self-hate	←————————→	Self-love to the exclusion of others
Self with Others:	Get what I want/need ←————→	Get what I do not want/need
Self with World:	Get what I want/need ←————→	Get what I do not want/need

Figure 3
Problem Analysis

respond. For some children, relationship with world or nature problems may also be expressed in spiritual terms. In such cases, the counselor may do well to listen for references to a deity that is understood by the child and parents to have power over all aspects of life. Listening for the child's point of relational reference as the problem is initially presented can be tremendously useful in that it provides an initial means for defining the nature of the child's presenting concern.

The second element in the definition of core issues holds that core issues are activated or triggered. When core issues are activated, they tend to generate problematic responses. Suggested in this part of the definition is the idea that core issue–related difficulties are not ever-present but rather are episodic and come into play under certain interpersonal or intrapersonal conditions or circumstances. Once the core issue is activated, the schema to which it is related will generate automatic thoughts, strong affect, and behavioral tendencies that tend to be maladaptive in nature (Young, 1990, 1999).

The third element in the definition of core issues is the idea that the child's responses to the issue tend to be evident over time. If a child is indeed struggling with one or more core issues, it would make sense that there would be patterns of responses consistent with these problems that can be traced from the present back over time. It would also hold that without appropriate intervention, that the pattern will likely continue into the future.

Young's Schema Domains and Early Maladaptive Schema Classifications

Recall that early maladaptive schemas are formed in response to thwarted attempts to meet one or more core emotional needs. Therefore, the identification of the core need(s) that was not sufficiently met at an early point in the child's life is a key element in both assessing the nature of a client's core issue and designing appropriate interventions. According to Young (1990, 1999) and Young et al. (2003), each of the five basic core emotional needs is associated with a different broad schema domain. A brief introduction of each domain is offered here to help ground the core issues framework.

The first of the schema domains is Disconnection and Rejection. This domain reflects a relational environment in which caregivers are not reliable in terms of providing for the core emotional needs of safety, security, love, and/or companionship. As a result, the child forms a relational worldview that relationships are unstable and that others will tend to disconnect or be rejecting.

The second is Impaired Autonomy and Performance. This domain is characterized by a relational environment that supports forms of emotional enmeshment or intrapersonal and interpersonal restraint. The core emotional needs at issue here are personal autonomy, competence, and a sense of identity. In this environment, the child receives messages that survival and well-being are not possible without continual guidance, direction, and advice.

The third is Impaired Limits, a domain that reflects the types of issues that arise when one has not learned to discern realistic limits and self-control. Individuals who encounter difficulties related to this domain usually experience relational environments in which limits are either overly rigid or overly lax in some respect. These children have trouble either responding adequately to the needs of others or fulfilling their own needs.

The fourth is Other-Directedness. This domain is characterized by an excessive emphasis on fulfilling the wants or emotional needs of others to the point that it becomes detrimental to one's self. Issues arise when the relational environment does not support or validate one's needs and emotions as being important. The basic frame of reference at work in this schema domain is that children might get emotional needs met, or at the very least avoid another's anger, if they make themselves constantly available to meet others' needs as opposed to their own.

The fifth is Overvigilance and Inhibition. This domain addresses the basic needs for pleasure, happiness, spontaneity, and expression. If the relational environment is such that it inhibits opportunities to experience happiness, the child may incorporate a worldview that tends to exclude any sense of joy or pleasure from life.

Figure 4 depicts the connection between the five core human needs and the five broad schema domains with which each is associated.

According to Young (1990, 1999) it is important to focus on the broad nature of the maladaptive schema domain during the initial phase of assessment. First, noting the schema domain helps in defining the broad categories of the child's struggle. Second, each domain characterizes the

Core Emotional Need Not Met	Associated Maladaptive Schema Domain
• Secure attachment to others	⟶ Disconnection and Rejection
• Autonomy, competence, and sense of identity	⟶ Impaired Autonomy and Performance
• Realistic limits and self-control	⟶ Impaired Limits
• Freedom to express valid needs and emotions	⟶ Other-Directedness
• Spontaneity of play	⟶ Overvigilance and Inhibition

Figure 4

Impact of Unmet Core Emotional Needs

broad goals that the child is striving to accomplish. Third, knowing the schema domain is helpful in providing a direction for the broad objectives of counseling that help the child achieve the goals that the maladaptive schema is blocking. Once the schema domain is identified, the counselor can focus on the specific early maladaptive schema that is at work as core issues in the child's life.

Recall once again how Young (1990, 1999) formulated the concept of early maladaptive schema core issues. According to Young, core issues form when an individual encounters relational interactions that fail to meet one or more core emotional needs on a continuous basis. Such relational encounters arising from repeated situations often generate considerable stress. If the child has the necessary resources to engage in problem-focused coping and to actually change the nature of the situational condition, it is likely that there will be very little lasting impact (Lazarus, 1991). However, if the child does not have either the resources or the power to engage successfully in problem-solving coping (a more likely scenario), the only other option is emotion-focused coping.

Early and continuous relationship encounters characterized by extremes can have a severe impact on a child's perception of the world. This is because when the only option one has is to continually engage in emotion-focused coping in response to maladaptive relational interactions, this will shape his or her relational view of self, others, and the world (Lazarus, 1991). The case study of John may aid in showing how the coping process generates a child's core issue.

John, 13 years of age, is the oldest of three children. His mother and father both work and do not get home during the week until after 6 p.m. John just completed an in-school babysitting course and holds a certificate required by law of any child older than the age of 12 who wishes to provide babysitting services. It was John's hope that he could earn extra money providing such services to families in his neighborhood. However, now that his parents can legally leave him to babysit, he is given responsibility for watching his two younger siblings, starting dinner, and doing household chores after school. John dislikes this situation because he is not allowed to join friends after school for play and sports activities. One might conclude that, because of his work responsibilities in the home environment, John's core emotional needs for spontaneity and play are being restricted.

John's coping process in response to this situational condition is activated in the following manner. A situational condition, in this case being held responsible for family tasks, exists as a stressor in John's life. He begins the coping process by cognitively construing the nature of the situational condition. Again, according to Lazarus (1991), the way in which a situation is construed depends largely on aspects of personality, goal commitments, beliefs, and knowledge. In this case, John construes the nature of this situational condition as being incongruent with his goals of interacting with his friends and engaging in after-school activities that are more to his liking. John next enters into a secondary appraisal process whereby he assesses the personal and social resources available to him in responding to the situation. John becomes aware of experiential outcomes, including a formulation of certain action tendencies, affect responses, and physiological experiences.

Feeling angry and frustrated, John now moves to coping options. At this point in his life, John has experienced a fair amount of success in dealing with environmental stressors head on. His secondary appraisal translates into taking the action of engaging in problem-solving coping with the hope that, if he is successful, the stressful situational condition will be alleviated. When his parents arrive home from work, John launches into an angry protest about having to be at home when his friends are outside enjoying their after-school hours. John's parents are unmoved by his protest. They explain that at a certain point everyone in the family is expected to make a contribution and that at 13 years of age John's time has come to help in the family effort. John protests and argues further, but his parents hold strong to their position. His parents' response puts John right up against a situational condition that, as it turns out, he is unsuccessful in changing. Because he is not successful in his attempts to change the situation and because the situation remains a present stressor, John must now use emotion-focused coping strategies. Again, engaging in emotion-focused coping requires an individual to rely on active psychological processes. John mobilizes his emotion-focused coping strategies to manage his cognitive, emotional, and physiological responses to the situational condition that he has appraised as a threat.

It should be made clear that John's situation is far from a worst case scenario. In fact, it might be viewed by some as an important character-building milestone that supports meeting one's responsibilities and contributing to family. However, it could also be argued that by placing too much responsibility on him, John's parents are restricting John's ability to develop normative peer relationships that evolve from after-school activities. Regardless of which position one takes on John's situation, the important point is that the process of emotion-focused coping impinges on an individual's beliefs; goal commitments; and knowledge about self, others, and the world. If an individual is exposed repeatedly to stressful relational encounters similar in nature, emotion-focused coping processes will over time reshape the relational schemas that organize his or her relational worldview.

Consider now more the severe circumstances that some individuals are forced to endure. Environments in which there is continual abuse, abandonment, or overprotection or in which children are held to unrelenting standards are but a few examples of environments in which emotion-focused coping strategies might need to be used. Children who are consistently in these environments will naturally form relational schemas that are consistent with the nature of the mistreatment. The relational schemas that are formed will reflect the negative relational experiences that are perpetuated in these less than ideal environments. Given that the schemas form within the context of negative relational experiences, it should be understandable that they will reflect the dysfunctional nature of that environment.

Appendix A lists each of the specific core issues associated with each of the five schema domains.

Summary

This chapter has addressed the fundamental concepts upon which the core issues perspective is built. The concept of emotion-focused coping in response to repeated exposure to relational environments in which core emotional needs are not adequately met was used to explain the process by which core issues originate.

Given that the processes involved in forming core issues take place within the context of an individual's relational environment, the cognitive schemas formed organize meaning regarding the relationship with self, others, and the world. When the relational environment to which one is repeatedly exposed does not support meeting one's core emotional needs, maladaptive relational schemas are formed. These maladaptive schemas, when triggered, organize information in a manner that results in particular thoughts, feelings, and behaviors that tend to be problematic in that person's current and past relational interactions. Chapter 3 builds on the principles presented thus far and examines the elements involved in conducting a core issues assessment.

early maladaptive schemas and associated schema domains

Disconnection and Rejection

The expectation that one's needs for security, safety, nurturance, empathy, sharing of feelings, acceptance, and respect will not be met in a predictable manner. Typically the family of origin is detached, cold, rejecting, withholding, lonely, explosive, unpredictable, or abusive.

1. **Abandonment/Instability**
   The perceived instability of those available for support and connection. Involves the sense significant others will not be able to continue to provide emotional support, connection, strength, or practical protection because they are emotionally unstable and unpredictable (e.g., prone to angry outbursts), unreliable, or erratically present; because they will die imminently; or because they will abandon the client for someone better.

2. **Mistrust/Abuse**
   The expectation that others will hurt, abuse, humiliate, cheat, lie, manipulate, or take advantage of the client. The schema usually involves the perception that the harm is intentional or the result of unjustified and extreme negligence. It may include the sense that one always ends up being cheated relative to others or "getting the short end of the stick."

3. **Emotional Deprivation**
   The expectation that one's desire for a normal degree of emotional support will not be adequately met by others. The three major forms of emotional deprivation are (a) deprivation of nurturance (absence of attention, affection, warmth, or companionship), (b) deprivation of empathy (absence of understanding, listening, self-disclosure, mutual sharing of feelings from others), and (c) deprivation of protection (absence of strength, direction, and/or guidance from others).

4. **Defectiveness/Shame**

The feeling that one is inwardly defective, bad, unwanted, inferior, or invalid in important respects or that one would be unlovable to significant others if exposed. This schema may involve hypersensitivity to criticism, rejection, and blame; self-consciousness, comparisons, and insecurity around others; or a sense of shame regarding one's perceived flaws. These flaws may be private (e.g., selfishness, angry impulses, unacceptable sexual desires) or public (e.g., undesirable physical appearance, social awkwardness).

5. **Social Isolation/Alienation**

The feeling that one is isolated from the rest of the world, different from other people, and/or not part of any group or community. This schema has to do more with how a client feels when in a group as opposed to with those who have been established as being emotionally close.

Impaired Autonomy and Performance

Expectations about one's self and the environment that interfere with one's perceived ability to separate, survive, function independently, or perform successfully. Typically the family of origin is enmeshed, undermines the child's confidence, is overprotective, or fails to reinforce the child for performing competently outside the family.

6. **Dependence/Incompetence**

The belief that one is unable to handle one's everyday responsibilities (e.g., taking care of oneself, solving daily problems, exercising good judgment, tackling new tasks, making good decisions) in a competent manner without considerable help from others. A client with this core issue will often present as helpless.

7. **Vulnerability to Harm or Illness**

The exaggerated fear that imminent catastrophe will strike at any time and one will be unable to prevent it. Fears focus on one or more of the following: (a) medical catastrophes (e.g., heart attacks, AIDS), (b) emotional catastrophes (e.g., going crazy), or (c) external catastrophes (e.g., elevators collapsing, victimization by a criminal, airplane crashes, earthquakes).

8. **Enmeshment/Undeveloped Self**

An excessive emotional involvement and closeness with one or more significant others (often the parents) at the expense of full individuation of normal social development. Often involves the belief that at least one of the enmeshed individuals cannot survive or be happy without the constant support of the other. May also include feelings of being smothered by, or fused with, others or insufficient individual identity. Often experienced as feeling empty and floundering, having no direction, or, in extreme cases, questioning one's existence. The parent often merges with the child and tries to limit differences between them. This creates a situation in which the child grows into an adult who has a sense that he or she cannot function without the person with whom he or she is enmeshed. The parent's message very likely was "We are one person and we must always be together." This creates a tremendous sense of guilt when the child has to separate. The client lives an existence that is largely an extension of the parent's.

9. **Failure**

    The belief that one has failed, will inevitably fail, or is fundamentally inadequate relative to one's peers in areas of achievement (school, career, sports, etc.). Often involves beliefs that one is stupid, inept, untalented, ignorant, lower in status, less successful than others, and so on.

Impaired Limits

A deficiency in internal limits, responsibility to others, or long-term goal orientation. Leads to difficulty respecting the rights of others, cooperating with others, making commitments, or setting and meeting realistic personal goals. Typically the family of origin is characterized by permissiveness, overindulgence, a lack of direction, or a sense of superiority rather than appropriate confrontation, discipline, and limits in relation to taking responsibility, cooperating in a reciprocal manner, and setting goals. In some cases, the child may not have been pushed to tolerate normal levels of discomfort or may not have been given adequate supervision, direction, or guidance.

10. **Entitlement/Grandiosity**

    The belief that one is superior to other people, entitled to special rights and privileges, or not bound by the rules of reciprocity that guide normal social interaction. Often involves an insistence that one should be able to do or have whatever one wants regardless of what is realistic, what others consider reasonable, or the cost to others; or an exaggerated focus of superiority (e.g., being among the most successful, famous, or wealthy) in order to achieve power and control (not primarily for attention or approval). Sometimes includes excessive competitiveness toward or domination of others: asserting one's power, forcing one's point of view, or controlling the behavior of others in line with one's own desires without empathy or concern for others' needs and feelings.

11. **Insufficient Self-Control/Self-Discipline**

    A pervasive difficulty or refusal to exercise sufficient and frustration tolerance to achieve one's personal goals or to restrain the excessive expression of one's emotions and impulses. In its milder form, it involves an exaggerated emphasis on discomfort avoidance: avoiding pain or conflict, confrontation, responsibility, or overexertion at the expense of personal fulfillment, commitment, or integrity.

Other-Directedness

An excessive focus on the desires, feelings, and responses of others at the expense of one's own needs in order to gain love and approval, maintain one's sense of connection, or avoid retaliation. Usually involves suppression and a lack of awareness regarding one's own anger and natural inclinations. Typically the family of origin is based on conditional acceptance: Children must suppress important aspects of themselves in order to gain love, attention, and approval. In many such families, the parents' emotional needs and desires—or social acceptance and status—are valued more than the unique needs and feelings of each child.

12. **Subjugation**

    The excessive surrendering of one's control to others—usually to avoid anger, retaliation, or abandonment—because one feels coerced. The two major forms of subjugation are (a) subjugation of needs (suppression of one's preferences, decisions, and desires) and (b) subjugation of emotions (suppression of emotional expression, especially anger). Usually involves the perception that one's own desires, opinions, and feelings are not valid or important to others. Frequently presents as excessive compliance, combined with hypersensitivity to feeling trapped. Generally leads to a buildup of anger manifested in maladaptive symptoms (e.g., passive-aggressive behavior, uncontrolled outbursts or temper, psychosomatic symptoms, withdrawal of affection, "acting out," substance abuse).

13. **Self-Sacrifice**

    An excessive focus on voluntarily meeting the needs of others in daily situations at the expense of one's own gratification. The most common reasons for doing this are to prevent pain to others, to avoid guilt from feeling selfish, and to maintain the connection with others as needy. Often results from an acute sensitivity to the pain of others. Sometimes leads to the sense that one's own needs are not being adequately met and to resentment of those who are being taken care of. (Overlaps with the concept of codependency.)

14. **Approval Seeking**

    An excessive emphasis on gaining approval, recognition, or attention from other people or fitting in at the expense of developing a secure and true sense of self. One's sense of esteem is dependent primarily on the reaction of others rather than on one's own natural inclinations. Sometimes includes an overemphasis on status, appearance, social acceptance, money, or achievement as means of gaining approval, administration, or attention (not primarily for power and control). Frequently results in major life decisions being made that are inauthentic or unsatisfying or in hypersensitivity to rejection.

Overvigilance and Inhibition

An excessive emphasis on suppressing one's spontaneous feelings, impulses, and choices or on meeting rigid internalized rules and expectations about performance and ethical behavior, often at the expense of happiness, self-expression, relaxation, close relationships, or health. Typically the family of origin is grim, demanding, and sometimes punitive: Performance, duty, perfection, following rules, hiding emotions, and avoiding mistakes predominate over pleasure, joy, and relaxation. There is usually an undercurrent of pessimism and worry that things could fall apart if one fails to be vigilant and careful at all times.

15. **Negativity and Pessimism**
    A pervasive and lifelong focus on the negative aspects of life (pain, death, loss, disappointment, conflict, guilt, resentment, unsolved problems, potential mistakes, betrayal, events that could go wrong, etc.) while minimizing or neglecting the positive or optimistic aspects of life. Usually includes an exaggerated expectation—in a wide range of work, financial, or interpersonal situations—that things will eventually go seriously wrong or that aspects of one's life that seem to be going well will ultimately fall apart. Usually involves an inordinate fear of making mistakes that might lead to financial collapse, loss, humiliation, or being trapped in a bad situation. Because potential negative outcomes are exaggerated, these clients are frequently characterized by chronic worry, vigilance, complaining, or indecision.

16. **Emotional Inhibition**
    The excessive inhibition of spontaneous action, feeling, or communication usually to avoid the disapproval of others, feelings of shame, or losing control of one's impulses. The most common areas of inhibition involve (a) the inhibition of anger; (b) the inhibition of positive impulses (e.g., joy, affection, sexual excitement, play); (c) difficulty expressing vulnerability or communicating freely about one's feelings, needs, and so on; or (d) an excessive emphasis on rationality while emotions are disregarded.

17. **Unrelenting Standards**
    The underlying belief that one must strive to meet very high internalized standards of behavior and performance, usually to avoid criticism. Typically results in feelings of pressure or difficulty slowing down and in being hypercritical toward oneself and others. Must involve significant impairment of pleasure, relaxation, health, self-esteem, sense of accomplishment, or satisfying relationships. Unrelenting standards typically present as (a) perfectionism, inordinate attention to detail, or an underestimation of how good one's own performance is relative to the norm; (b) rigid rules and "shoulds" in many areas of life, including unrealistically high moral, ethical, cultural, or religious precepts; or (c) preoccupation with time and efficiency so that more can be accomplished.

18. **Punitiveness**

The belief that people should be harshly punished for making mistakes. Involves the tendency to be angry, intolerant, punitive, and impatient with those people (including oneself) who do not meet one's expectations or standards. Usually includes having difficulty forgiving mistakes in oneself or others because of a reluctance to consider extenuating circumstances, allow for human imperfection, or empathize with the feelings of others.

Note. Copyright 2003 by Jeffrey E. Young, PhD, director of the Schema Therapy Institute. Adapted with permission. Unauthorized reproduction without written consent of the author is prohibited. For more information, write Cognitive Therapy Center of New York, 36 West 44th Street, Suite 1007, New York, NY 10036; see also http://www.schematherapy.com/cognitive/id342.htm.

assessment of core issues and the nature of the child's living story

This chapter provides an overview of how the counselor progresses through the five specific tasks involved in completing an assessment of a child's core issues. Also introduced in this chapter is the concept of the child's living story. One's living story is best described as the real-time narrative that is lived out in vivo and serves as the underpinnings for a worldview from which relational meaning making is constructed (Halstead, 2007). Establishing an empathic understanding of the client's living story orients the counselor as to where there may be pockets of personal dysfunction and provides avenues for therapeutic resolution.

Conducting any thorough assessment requires applying a number of counseling skills in a methodical manner. If the assessment is successful, the counselor will be able to formulate a clear conceptualization of the client, the nature of the client's problem, and the root cause of that problem. Children, who may have a limited ability to express the nature of their discomfort, often present with difficulties that are layered in complex ways. Therefore, it can be a major challenge to establish a basic understanding of where to begin and what aspects of the child's life to focus on. Consider the following story.

A number of years ago, while a graduate student, one of us was involved in a supervision group session with his primary supervisor and two other counseling interns. It was early in the semester, and this was the first time he was to present a client he had met the previous day to conduct an intake interview and assessment. In reporting the client's early history in supervision, he used a standard statement often found in textbooks: "This client seems to have had a very normal childhood with no remarkable emotional or psychological events." Upon hearing this statement, the supervisor held up his hand, stopping him. As he was about to find out, this particular supervisor was extremely skilled at creating intense learning experiences in supervision. This supervisor was a master at composing a moment within which important learning would take place in a manner that often had a profound impact on his supervisees. In this instance, he paused for what seemed like a very long time with a locked gaze. The moment was tense, and this supervisee was not sure what it was that had caught his supervisor's attention. The other interns looked down at the floor to avoid drawing attention to themselves. Then, in a barely audible voice, the supervisor said, "Childhood, no matter how normal it may appear, is always a difficult emotional and psychological struggle. Each of us who has made it to adulthood has had to survive our respective childhoods. It is the counselor's job to help the client give a voice to the experience of that struggle" (J. R. Wilett, personal communication, September 22, 1985). The supervisor then sat silently for another moment, allowing his statement to have its full effect.

Understanding that all children, no matter what, are engaged in a struggle is a key element in realizing the value of applying the core issues framework. Assessing the nature of a child's core issues helps the counselor to define the material that children often have difficulties expressing. It is this material that can be the focus of the assessment and serves as a basis to inform the counseling intervention.

Developmental Factors

Central to the human experience is the range of experiences associated with relational connectedness to self, others, and the world. Understanding the long-term nature and quality of a child's relational connectedness is at the center of conducting a core issues assessment. This perspective presupposes that, given enough time, everyone will eventually experience some level of difficulty with relationship encounters. It is clear that some forms of abusive treatment can cause serious emotional and psychological harm, but many other less traumatic experiences can also create problems for a child. Experiences such as loss, betrayal, abandonment, or being overprotected are just a few examples of relational encounters that can lead to maladaptive core issues. These types of experiences may occur for many different reasons throughout a child's life. In some cases, the hurts suffered in relationships have long-lasting effects and result in low self-esteem, repressed feelings, destructive patterns of behavior, difficulty trusting others, and a whole host of unwanted feelings.

Even under the best of conditions, children will endure difficulties that are simply part of childhood. Two elements work in tandem to generate these difficulties. First is how the child is treated by others relative to having his or her basic needs met. If the child is deprived of the emotional connection needed or is treated in a manner that is directly hurtful, such as in the case of physical abuse, relationally oriented difficulties may result. Second is the limited control children have over their environment (Parry & Doan, 1994). As a result of having this limited control, children must become adept at assessing their environments and developing strategies to adjust and adapt to that which they encounter in their young lives. On one level, the struggles of childhood can be understood as instrumental to a child's psychosocial development. If it were not for various problematic situational conditions to which they must attend, it is unlikely that children would develop the broad array of socially oriented coping skills necessary for successful growth and coping. In fact, many children are able to build strong coping skills in the relational arena that allow them to adjust well to the many perils of childhood. Although the skills that are developed as a result of rising to challenging situational conditions are clearly beneficial, this form of psychosocial learning can also result in a child developing a problematic relational worldview that is consistent with one or more core issues.

A child who is fortunate enough to have been born into a family with loving and supportive parents still faces many difficult challenges. Conflicts with siblings, failure at school tasks, normal physical challenges, and negotiating peer group relationships all require varying degrees of emotion-focused coping. The situation is much more challenging for children who grow up in environments in which physical boundaries are violated, there is constant criticism, there is an absence of emotional caring, or there are any number of other extremely difficult relationally oriented events. Relational experiences that fail to meet important core emotional needs can evoke a variety of unwanted feelings. Difficult relational situations that do not respond to problem-focused coping efforts must be handled through a process of emotion-focused coping. The emotion-focused coping processes involved in managing those relational challenges shape the nature of the core issues that develop and that the child may be forced to deal with later in life. In this sense, core issues can be thought of as primary story themes that children act out in their day-to-day relationships with self, others, and the world. The degree of impairment with which a child may struggle in acting out his or her core issues story is usually determined by the severity of the environment and the degree to which relational challenges are consistent over extended periods of time.

Conducting a Core Issues Assessment

The core issues framework greatly aids in the assessment process because it helps the counselor focus on the basic elements of the core problem that children often have difficulty expressing through verbal communication. Assessing a child's core issues involves several tasks that draw on the clinician's ability to understand, analyze, synthesize, and evaluate many aspects of interacting with a relational environment. Following a structured procedure is always helpful when tackling the complex task of assessment. This is especially true when a counselor is conducting a core issues assessment because of the individualized nature of core issues and the manner in which these issues may be expressed in a child's life.

Five essential tasks are involved in completing a core issues assessment: (a) exploring the child's presenting problem, (b) generating initial core issues hypotheses, (c) tracing the child's psychosocial history to test the validity of core issues hypotheses, (d) assessing the child's response style to the core issues, and (e) establishing a full core issues conceptualization. Each task must be done carefully and completely to ensure an accurate assessment of the core issues and how they become active in the child's life.

Assessment Task 1:
Exploring the Child's Presenting Problem

The initial phase in conducting a core issues assessment involves gathering information about the child's presenting problem and discerning how severe its impact is in his or her life. This phase of the assessment deviates little from the standard mental health intake format used with children in many counseling settings. The counselor should be active in obtaining information from the child, parents or caregivers, and school personnel. Key elements of focus should be the child's current level of functioning, the presence of any harm risk, as well as the child's biological and psychosocial history. It is important to conduct a thorough assessment that meets the ethical and legal obligations of practice within the standard of care established by the profession (Corey et al., 2007; Madden, 1998). As previously stated, the core issues framework is a complementary adjunct to standard diagnostic procedures, not a replacement for those procedures. A standard intake interview form is provided in Appendix B.

During this first phase of core issues assessment, the counselor needs to pay special attention to the relational context within which the problem is being presented. In other words, which of the three types of relationships within the relational triad is being identified as problematic? Does the presenting problem and the underlying issue pertain to a relationship with self, others, or the world? Although the identified problem can shift over time as the core issue becomes clearer, it is important to note at which point in the relational triad the child's problem is most focused at the time of intake. Understanding the initial relational framing of the problem enables the counselor to more readily engage in empathic reflection, which enhances rapport building early in the counseling relationship. For example, a child displeased with one or more characteristics of himself or herself is focused on the "relationship with self" portion of the relational triad; this focus provides the counselor with a frame of reference for initial responses.

The counselor must also consider the presenting problem in the broader context of the child's life at the present time. During this step the counselor begins to think about differentiating the identified problem from the child's response to that problem. It is helpful during this assessment phase to remember that the problematic issues in a child's life often reflect multiple interconnected problems. It is, therefore, quite easy for the counselor to become confused by the many details of the problem that may be presented. During the early phases of assessment it is useful to mentally organize the information the client provides. This is most easily done by placing information into broad categories. Prompt the child and caregivers to share why counseling is being requested. The initial response to this inquiry will either provide information about some sort of identified "problem" situation (e.g., the death of a loved one, difficulty with classmates, poor academic performance) or provide some form of response to the problem (e.g., sadness, hurt, anger, depression, or anxiety). It is important for the counselor to determine the degree to which the child understands the full scope of both the problem and how he or she is responding to that problem. Helping the child make this distinction is important because many times what it presented as the problem is just the first layer of a larger problematic picture. In addition, what the client presents as the problem might be more accurately described, from a more objective perspective, as a response to a more primary causal problem, or core issue. The case of Monica illustrates this point.

The Case of Monica

Monica is an energetic, bright-eyed, biracial (African American and Caucasian) child. At 6 years of age, Monica has already had many unpleasant and some traumatic experiences. Monica was in foster care for nearly a year after she and her younger sister were removed from their biological mother's home because of neglect. According to the Department of Social Services caseworker who was handling Monica's case, Monica had been burned by her mother as a form of punishment. The transition into foster care was not terribly difficult for Monica, as she was respectful and well behaved. However, Monica has recently begun to present with some problematic behaviors at school and at home. She has what are described as frequent angry outbursts in which she becomes physically aggressive with others and, at times, self-injurious. The trigger for her anger is not easily identified by members of her foster care family or the school. In addition, her teacher has expressed that Monica's inability to stay on task has gotten progressively worse and that any interventions she has used to help Monica focus are met with inappropriate comments and language directed at the teacher. The foster care parents also note that Monica sleeps little and expresses fear and worry about her younger sister.

This case study provides ample data to begin the first task in the process of a core issues assessment, that of exploring the presenting problem. The counselor who is working from a core issues perspective will wonder about the set of problems with which Monica presents. Is there any evidence of a more global problematic pattern? If so, when and under what conditions is the pattern triggered? What more basic issue or problem could explain the difficulties with which Monica now struggles?

From a core issues perspective, the information gathered about Monica thus far suggests that the counselor has not yet been made privy to Monica's "problem" but rather her "response" to the problem. To understand Monica's problem the counselor needs to explore additional information that will eventually lead to a deeper understanding of her core struggle.

Monica's psychosocial history reveals that along with feelings of anger, she has also experienced elements related to the core issues of abandonment, abuse, and emotional deprivation. By probing for information and considering how it might fit into a core issues framework, the counselor begins to understand Monica's behavior within the context of a larger picture of possible causes for her pattern of problematic behavior. This information is used to establish a number of important distinctions regarding Monica's problem and her response to that problem. First, the relational context of Monica's initial presenting problem (e.g., angry statements, acts of physical aggression, verbal assaults) seems to be consistent with a problem with others. Second, the problem reported may actually be a response to the more fundamental problem of Monica being unable to establish a sense of trust in those around her as well as needing to maintain control in whatever primitive manner she can given her limited personal and social resources. Making these distinctions enables the counselor to focus the next step of the assessment more accurately and helps to ensure a clearer identification of Monica's core issue.

Assessment Task 2:
Generating Initial Core Issues Hypotheses

Once the counselor has made an initial distinction between the client's problem and the client's response to that problem, the counselor must ask "What is the cause of the client's problem?" This is the key core issues question. To answer this question, the counselor constructs a thorough psychosocial history and compares that information with the thematic frames of core issue domains and individual core issues first identified by Young (1999). This is a two-step process that involves first generating hypotheses of what the potential core issues might be and then testing the validity of those hypotheses.

For example, in this phase of the assessment, the counselor engages in an active process of hypothesizing the cause of Monica's problem by examining the core issues that stand a good chance of generating the symptoms that present themselves as problematic. By actively tracing Monica's relational history and exploring the various points when she may have engaged in emotion-focused coping, the counselor can move toward pinpointing the core elements to which Monica is responding. The counselor pays special attention to how Monica's emotion-focused coping may have fostered her interaction style with those around her. Specifically, the counselor attends to the nature of Monica's past relational environments and the conditions she was exposed to over time that may be consistent with one or more core issues. A brief description of a play therapy session with Monica is provided here to illustrate how one might engage in hypothesizing the presence of possible core issues.

Play therapy is used as the initial modality because of Monica's age and her limited ability to verbally articulate what triggers her angry outbursts. In this first session Monica takes an immediate interest in the play therapy room, as evidenced by her wide smile. Monica engages in some exploration of the playroom but stays in unusually close proximity to the counselor. Using a child-centered approach to play therapy, the counselor begins by inviting Monica to do *almost* anything and say anything in the playroom. Monica explores all of the toys while smiling and maintaining a high level of eye contact with the play therapist. She invites the counselor to play catch with her. Monica makes it very challenging for the counselor. For example, Monica purposely throws the ball to the counselor's feet, throws the ball exceptionally hard or high, or does "trick" throws (pretends to throw the ball but does not). She smiles and says "yes" as the counselor makes reflective responses such as "You are really proud that you tricked me. It feels good to be the one who decides how to play."

This short snippet between Monica and her counselor reveals one more bit of information about this little girl. When given the opportunity, Monica provides information as to where problems might exist in her relational world. Although each element of her response is important, certain responses would draw attention from a core issues perspective. For example, Monica maintains almost constant eye contact with the counselor during their interaction. This stands out as being inconsistent with the normative behavior of other 6-year-old children when they are first exposed to a room full of play items. Moreover, Monica's ball play with the counselor communicates that she has some need to control her interactions with others. She controls the ball play by making it difficult, if not impossible, for the counselor to participate in the game. She delights in her control and perhaps wants to feel powerful. This play interaction matches earlier reports from teachers that Monica's interactions with others are often aggressive and manipulative. The counselor must consider the nature of this information within the context of Monica's psychosocial history and any broad core issue domains that may apply.

Assessment Task 3:
Tracing the Child's Psychosocial History to Test the Validity of Core Issues Hypotheses

A core issues assessment must be made cautiously. The counselor should never rush to judgment about the existence of any one particular core issue early in the assessment process. Rather, the counselor should use information collected in the interview first to build a preliminary core issues hypothesis and then to test the validity of that hypothesis, or lack thereof, with additional information. An intervention focused on the wrong core issue is likely to be relatively ineffective (Halstead, 2007; Young et al., 2003). Particular elements of Monica's presentation are significant from a core issues perspective, and these elements can be used to begin building a preliminary hypothesis about Monica's story.

Two key pieces of information emerge from Monica's story. First, there is some evidence that Monica's early relational environment was harsh. Given that she was removed from her mother's "care" by the Department of Social Services because of neglect and severe punishment, one can hypothesize an initial core issue domain of Disconnection and Rejection

(Young, Weinberger, & Beck, 2001). Growing up in a neglectful and abusive relational environment, Monica was required to cope with the threat of emotional and physical neglect as well as harm. Her mother deprived her of a sense of safety, love, and acceptance. As a result, Monica quite understandably might carry with her some level of mistrust and yet still have a desire to connect. Children who are exposed to environments of abuse and neglect must find effective emotion-focused coping strategies to help them survive. The second key piece of information from Monica's story comes from the exchange she has with her counselor during their first play therapy session. Monica's nonnormative tendency to maintain unbroken eye contact and her efforts to gain control within the play environment are markers of her core issue(s).

Caution must be exercised in reaching a definitive conclusion regarding a child's core issue(s). The counselor needs to constantly be aware of new information that may emerge that would either further validate the core issues hypothesis or suggest that a different core issue is at the center of the client's struggle. However, given the information gathered from and about Monica thus far, one would have reasonable evidence to suggest that Monica's problem falls within the broad problematic domain known as Disconnection and Rejection and involves the specific core issues of abandonment/instability, mistrust/abuse, and deprivation of nurturance.

According to Young et al. (2003), a client who has been blocked from meeting basic emotional and safety needs will often exhibit struggles within the Disconnection and Rejection core issue domain. Young et al. (2003) suggested that the Disconnection and Rejection domain pertains to relational environment conditions in which one's expectation for security, safety, nurturance, empathy, sharing of feelings, acceptance, and respect are not met in a predictable manner. In such cases, the family of origin is detached, cold, rejecting, withholding, explosive, unpredictable, or abusive. The core issues with which Monica initially presents include the following elements:

- *Abandonment/instability.* The perceived instability of those available to the client for support and connection. This core issue involves the sense that significant others will not continually provide emotional support, connection, strength, or practical protection because they are emotionally unstable, unpredictable, unreliable, or erratically present and they will abandon the client.
- *Mistrust/abuse.* The expectation that others will hurt, abuse, humiliate, cheat, lie, manipulate, or take advantage of the client or his or her situation. Usually, this schema involves the perception that the harm is intentional or the result of unjustified and extreme negligence. It may include the sense that one always ends up being cheated relative to others.
- *Emotional deprivation.* The expectation that one's desire for a normal degree of emotional support will not be adequately met by others. The three major forms of emotional deprivation are (a) deprivation

of nurturance (absence of attention, affection, warmth, or companionship), (b) deprivation of empathy (absence of understanding, listening, self-disclosure, mutual sharing of feelings from others), and (c) deprivation of protection (absence of strength, direction, and/or guidance from loved ones).

Assessment Task 4:
Assessing the Child's Response Style to the Core Issues

Once the counselor has conducted a full psychosocial assessment to establish the initial hypotheses about the possible core issue(s) the child may be presenting, the next task is to understand the child's specific expressions of the core issue(s). One way to think about core issues is to conceptualize them as thematic presentations of a child's core issues story. The specific responses the client exhibits frame the manner in which the child lives out that core story. These specific responses illustrate the child's strategy for responding to the core issue when it is triggered. Upon being exposed to any situational condition, an individual will engage in a process of appraising the nature of the situational condition as well as the personal resources he or she has developed for dealing with the situation. As a result of this appraisal process, the individual will engage in either problem-focused or emotion-focused coping (Lazarus, 1991), as described in Chapter 2.

Within these two broad coping strategy categories are individually specific coping styles. Over time, a number of models have attempted to capture specific coping styles. Gladstone (1955) suggested seven styles of response options to a threatening stressor: counterthreat, attack, defend, compliance, defiance, avoidance, and circumvention. Carver et al. (1989) proposed 15 individually specific coping behaviors: active coping, planning, suppression of competing activities, positive reinterpretation, restraint from action, seeking instrumental social support, seeking emotional social support, religion or spiritual support, humor, acceptance, focusing on and venting emotions, denial, mental disengagement, behavioral disengagement, and alcohol/drug use. Building on the work of Carver and colleagues, Zuckerman and Gagne (2003) specified five dimensions of coping based on analyzing the factor structure as well as convergent and discriminant validity of coping measures. These five dimensions are self-help, approach, accommodation, avoidance, and self-punishment.

Three basic themes would emerge in a content analysis of the coping dimensions across these three models: (a) a tendency to resist or fight against the threat, (b) a tendency to avoid the threat, and (c) a tendency to give in or surrender to the threat. Those familiar with adaptive reactions to stressful conditions may recognize the first two of these broad response styles as those popularized as the "fight-or-flight response." When confronted with a threatening situational condition, an individual's autonomic nervous system will physiologically prepare the individual either to stand and fight or to quickly move away from the threat. M. E. Seligman (1975) expanded on the idea of a fight-or-flight response when he advanced the concept known as *learned helplessness*. Seligman observed that when an animal is exposed to a painful shock and has no means of stopping or avoiding that stimulus, the animal will surrender and endure the painful stimulus in a helpless manner. Seligman then generalized the concept of learned helplessness and surrender as a psychological dynamic applicable to a variety of human struggles. Drawing on the stress and threat literature, Young et al. (2003) suggested that three coping response styles can be expressed in response to a core issue threat. From a core issues perspective, a *threat* is a relational condition that triggers some sense within an individual that a core emotional need will go unmet as it did during earlier formative periods of life (Young, 1999). When the core issue threat is triggered, the individual experiences a flood of intense thoughts and feelings and responds with one of three primary coping responses. Young (1999) labeled these coping responses *compensation adaptation*, *avoidance adaptation*, and *surrender adaptation*. Each of these responses to a stressful situational condition can be adaptive, depending on the specific circumstances of the situation. For example, Wrosch, Scheier, Carver, and Schulz (2003) advanced the idea that the action of goal disengagement, a form of avoidance response, can be adaptive in that it allows an individual to redirect energies in new directions that ultimately may serve the individual better over the longer term. Young et al. (2003) pointed out that when taken to an extreme, any coping style becomes maladaptive. For example, an individual confronted with particular personal deficits might try to compensate for specific weaknesses by focusing more on strengths to counter those weaknesses. However, this coping response becomes maladaptive when the person begins to overcompensate for a deficit by demanding personal perfection in everything and everyone. This type of overcompensation response is likely to create some form of difficulty for the individual over time. Maladaptive coping styles can become incorporated in the problematic core issue generated in response to situations that arise in the client's life.

To better understand these coping response styles from a core issues perspective, consider again 6-year-old Monica. Assume for the moment that the initial core issues hypotheses of mistrust/abuse, abandonment/instability, and emotional deprivation are valid for this child. Given the three coping processes (i.e., compensation adaptation, avoidance adaptation, and surrender adaptation), one would rightly surmise that Monica's response to her core issues would in fact vary based on the form of adaptation that she uses in her attempts to cope with her internal experience. A compensation adaptation might find her being more socially outgoing or perhaps aggressive. An avoidance adaptation could be expressed as turning inward and becoming more withdrawn and sullen. Surrender adaptation in Monica's case would carry with it a tendency to provoke others in a manner that might draw them into either hurting her (abuse) and/or withdrawing, thus leaving her alone (abandonment and emotionally isolation).

Information from her history as well as her initial session shows Monica very much engaged in efforts to take control and in some cases to exercise overt aggression toward others. Again, the core issue domain that best characterizes Monica's relational family life is Disconnection and Rejection. Within this domain, the hypothesis that best captures her core issues is abandonment/instability, mistrust/abuse, and emotional deprivation. These core issues are best characterized by a relational worldview in which people are not consistently reliable or are unavailable for support. Monica might exhibit any one of the three coping modalities in response to this abandonment core issue. She could try to compensate for her feelings of abandonment, try to avoid relationships to keep from feeling abandoned, or to surrender to her feeling of abandonment.

Compensation Adaptation

When an individual overcompensates for a core issue, this coping response can result in a problematic pattern that interferes with goal attainment. For example, if Monica were to use a compensation coping strategy, she would likely respond to her abandonment by reaching out to others and thus overcompensate for the loss of her mother. Her abandonment core issue would predispose her to experiencing a sense of abandonment whenever there was some uncertainty regarding the stability of her relational environment. Once triggered, Monica's abandonment core issue would mobilize a pattern of problematic emotional responses. Feeling that she might be left alone again, she might begin to express her neediness and want reassurance that others will stand by her, or she might be overly aggressive and controlling (as seen in the session snippet above). As her needs escalate, Monica might be experienced by others as very needy, clingy, or overly aggressive. As a result, others might distance themselves emotionally, which would leave Monica feeling abandoned yet again and longing even more for a close emotional connection. This cycle would then repeat itself.

Avoidance Adaptation

Avoidance adaptation is characterized by cognitive, affective, or behavioral patterns that enable the child to in some sense avoid a stressful relational situational condition. The child's energies are mobilized to either minimize discomfort or avoid experiencing discomfort if at all possible. If Monica were to use an avoidance adaptation to her abandonment core issue, she would likely close herself off from others and not allow herself to become emotionally close to anyone. She would develop a style that is more withdrawn and would work to avoid interactions with others.

Surrender Adaptation

Surrender adaptation is characterized by the individual giving in to the core issue. The child identifies with the characteristic elements of the core issue and accepts a role consistent with what the core issue expresses. Monica might express a surrender adaptation by not feeling deserving or worthy of having a close connection with others. She might develop an internal perspective tantamount to "I am the person whom others will leave behind. I get very sad about it, but that is who I am and that is all I can ever really expect." Working from this particular coping strategy, Monica would engage others who have a more emotionally distant tone to their presentation and who are likely over time to become distant. When there is a failure to connect or maintain the connection, the core issue is reinforced.

Assessing a child's response style when a particular core issue is triggered can help the counselor develop a sense of the child's strategy for coping with the thoughts and feelings that any core issue will generate. An assessment of a client's response style also serves to explain what motivates the client's response behaviors.

Assessment Task 5:
Establishing a Full Core Issues Conceptualization

In the previous phases of the assessment process, the counselor conducts an initial exploration of the child's presenting problem, generates an initial hypothesis about the child's core issue themes, traces the child's psychosocial history to determine his or her response style, and finally works toward testing the validity of the core issues hypotheses. The final step in the assessment process is to arrive at an overall conceptualization of the child and the nature of the current struggle. This last step involves pulling all of the elements of the assessment together to form a synthesized whole that expresses the nature of the core emotional need that is surmised to have gone unmet, the specific core issue with which the client struggles, and the manner in which the core issue is expressed.

A full and accurate case conceptualization serves as the basis for generating short- and long-term outcome goals and guides implementation of the counseling plan and associated interventions. Table 3 illustrates the coping style and relational orientation assessment model for each of the core issues. It is important to filter the content of the child's story through these coping processes so that the nature of the relational struggle with the self, others, or the world can be adequately addressed.

As the counselor continues to gather information and listen to the nature of the core issue the child presents, a full clinical picture should emerge. The counselor can state with a degree of certainty which core emotional need the child has had difficulty meeting and, based on a case history, the core issue(s) with which the child is struggling and the response style used during times of relational stress. A relationally oriented clinical focus toward assessment addresses with whom or with what the problematic core issue is relationally associated in the client's life: self, others, or the world. This model presupposes that each of these three elements across the dimensions of coping style and relational focus are always present, function in combination with one another, and can be identified for a richer and more complete clinical description (see Figure 5).

Monica has internalized a set of core issues (abandonment/instability, mistrust/abuse, emotional deprivation), and as a result the relational focus of her presented problem is her interaction with others. When her core issue is triggered it evokes a compensation response characterized by overly aggressive and controlling interactions.

Table 3

The Coping Style and Relational Orientation Assessment Model

Early Adaptive Schema	Examples of Compensation	Examples of Avoidance	Examples of Surrender
Abandonment/ Instability	Clings to and will smother friends and caring adults, driving them away; becomes angry over even a minor separation	Avoids intimate relationships; plays alone; develops a connection to solitary activities (video games)	Chooses friends who do not offer a connection emotionally or physically but remains in the relationship
Mistrust/Abuse	Uses and abuses others; bullies ("get others before they get you")	Avoids becoming vulnerable; keeps secrets	Engages in repetition and compulsion; puts self in a vulnerable position in a relationship
Emotional Deprivation	Acts emotionally demanding with family and close friends	Avoids intimate relationships altogether	Selects emotionally depriving friends and does not ask them to meet needs
Defectiveness/ Shame	Criticizes and rejects others while seeming to be perfect, bossy, and a know-it-all	Avoids expressing true thoughts and feelings and letting others get close	Selects critical and rejecting friends; puts self down
Social Isolation/ Alienation	Becomes a chameleon to fit into groups	Avoids social situations and groups; may be "unknown" to classmates	In social situations, including school, focuses exclusively on differences from others rather than similarities
Dependence/ Incompetence	Does not ask anyone for anything ("I can do it myself")	Avoids taking on new challenges that get in the way of academic and social tasks	Asks parents, family, and friends to make all decisions
Vulnerability to Harm or Illness	Acts recklessly, without regard to danger; is counterphobic	Avoids going places that do not seem totally safe; has difficulty separating from others	Thinks obsessively about catastrophes and anticipates them in everyday situations
Enmeshment/ Undeveloped Self	Tries to become different from family members, especially siblings and parents	Avoids intimacy; stays dependent	Tells mother everything; lives through siblings, parents, and friends or peers

(Continued)

Table 3 (*Continued*)
The Coping Style and Relational Orientation Assessment Model

Early Adaptive Schema	Examples of Compensation	Examples of Avoidance	Examples of Surrender
Failure	Becomes an overachiever by ceaselessly driving himself or herself	Avoids academic challenges completely; procrastinates on tasks	Does tasks in a halfhearted or haphazard manner and seems lazy
Entitlement/ Grandiosity	Attends excessively to the needs of others	Avoids situations in which he or she is average, not superior	Bullies others into getting own way; brags about own accomplishments
Insufficient Self-Control/ Self-Discipline	Becomes overly self-controlled or self-disciplined	Avoids academic or leadership responsibility	Gives up easily on routine tasks
Subjugation	Rebels against authority	Avoids situations that might involve conflict with another individual	Lets other individuals control situations and make choices
Self-Sacrifice	Gives as little as possible to others	Avoids situations that involve giving or taking	Gives a lot to others and asks for nothing in return
Approval Seeking	Goes out of the way to provoke the disapproval of others; stays in the background	Avoids interacting with those whose approval is coveted	Acts to impress others
Negativity and Pessimism	Is overly optimistic or "Pollyanna"; like and denies unpleasant realities	Blots out pessimistic feelings and unhappiness	Focuses on the negative; ignores the positive; worries constantly; goes to great lengths to avoid any possible negative outcome

(Continued)

Table 3 (*Continued*)
The Coping Style and Relational Orientation Assessment Model

Early Adaptive Schema	Examples of Compensation	Examples of Avoidance	Examples of Surrender
Emotional Inhibition	Awkwardly tries to be the center of attention, even though forced and unnatural	Avoids situations in which people discuss or express feelings; does not know feeling words	Maintains an emotionally calm and flat demeanor
Unrelenting Standards	Does not care about standards; does tasks in a hasty, careless manner	Avoids or procrastinates in situations and on tasks in which performance will be judged	Spends inordinate amounts of time trying to be perfect
Punitiveness	Behaves in an overly forgiving way	Avoids others for fear of punishment	Treats self and others in a harsh, punitive manner

Note. Adapted for application to children from Table 1.1. *Examples of Maladaptive Coping Responses* in *Schema Therapy: A Practitioner's Guide* (pp. 38–39), by J. E. Young, J. S. Klosko, and M. E. Weishaar, 2003, New York, NY: Guilford Press. Copyright 2003 by The Guilford Press. Reprinted with permission.

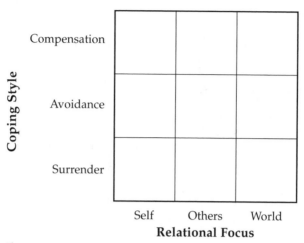

Figure 5

The Coping Style and Relational Orientation Assessment Model

At this point in conducting an assessment of Monica's struggle, the counselor should be able to provide a rather complete clinical description. The counselor should be able to state with a degree of certainty the core emotional need that was difficult for Monica to meet and, based on her reported history, Monica's struggles with specific core issues. As depicted in Figure 6, when Monica's core issues are triggered, it evokes troublesome thoughts and feelings to which she responds by using a compensation adaptation directed specifically toward others in her relational sphere.

With a full descriptive conceptualization in place, the counselor is better able to design an intervention that not only incorporates attention to Monica's behaviors but also addresses the core elements that are central to her problem of engaging in more prosocial interactions with the relational environment.

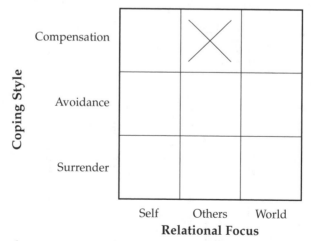

Figure 6

Monica's Identified Coping Style and Relational Orientation

Summary

This chapter has presented an assessment process that consists of five different but related tasks. The first task is to conduct an initial exploration of the child's presenting problem. This initial exploration deviates little from what is usually done when counseling children. The counselor's goal is to obtain information pertaining to the child's current level of functioning, the presence of any risk of harm, and the child's biological and psychosocial history. The counselor should also work to make an initial distinction between the child's problem and the child's response to that problem.

The second task in the assessment process is to generate an initial core issues hypothesis. The core issues are identified by comparing the child's psychosocial history with information in the thematic frames of core issue domains and individual core issue elements. This process is a gradual one and involves first generating hypotheses about potential core issues for the child and then testing the validity of those hypotheses.

The third task is to trace the child's psychosocial history to test the validity of the core issues hypotheses. A core issues assessment must be made cautiously; the counselor should never rush to judgment about the existence of any one particular core issue. Rather, the counselor must use information collected in the interview first to build a preliminary core issues hypothesis and then to test the validity of that hypothesis using additional historical information. An intervention focused on the wrong core issue is likely to be ineffective.

The fourth task is to assess the client's response or coping style when a particular core issue is triggered. This involves working toward an understanding of the client's individual responses and expressions of the core issue. Three different responses or adaptations to core issues are compensation adaptation, avoidance adaptation, and surrender adaptation.

The fifth task is to synthesize the information that has been collected and articulate the nature of the core emotional need that has gone unmet, the specific core issue with which the child struggles, and the manner in which the core issue is expressed. The child's coping style describes the nature of that child's response to the problem; the relational focus addresses with whom or with what the problematic core issue is relationally associated. Once this final step in the assessment process is completed, the counselor can design an intervention that not only incorporates the child's initial problematic concern but also addresses the core elements central to generating the problem and motivating behavior.

counseling intake and assessment form

Date: _____ Parent/Guardian Phone #: _____

Child's Name: _____ Child's Gender: _____

Address: _____ Age: _____

_____

Ethnicity and race: _____

Presenting Problem(s)

Duration of the presenting problem: _____

_____

History of the presenting problem and/or similar problems in the past: _____

_____

_____

Risk Assessment

Current or past ideation of harmful behaviors (suicide and homicide): _____

_____

Intention to take action on thoughts of harming self or others: _____

_____

Specificity of plan(s): _____

_____

Availability of means: _____

_____

Lethality of method: _____

_____

History of harmful behaviors (self, relatives, friends, etc.): _____

_____

Client History

Significant developmental milestones: _____

_____

History of interpersonal relationships (include quality of peer relationships,

significant losses, separations, etc.): _____

_____

Academic history (include any remarkable indicators such as being developmentally gifted, developmental delays, learning disabilities, etc.): _____

_____

History self-abusive behaviors: _____

_____

History of sexual abuse (past or present, nature and duration, abuse of other family members, any warning signs or indicators of abuse in current relationship,
etc.): _____

_____

History of previous counseling: ☐Yes ☐No

If yes, when, with whom (name[s] and phone number[s] of past counselor[s]),
what issues were addressed, and will client give a release to contact the former
counselor? _____

_____

List psychiatric medications and dosage presently or in the past: _____

_____

Health Status *(any history of health problems)*

Date of last physical exam: _____

History of medical conditions and/or current health status: _____

_____

Nonpsychiatric medications: ☐No ☐Yes

Name(s) of medication(s):_____ Dose _____

_____ Dose _____

_____ Dose _____

_____ Dose _____

_____ Dose _____

_____ Dose _____

54

Mental Status Assessment
I. Social Presentation
Appearance

Grooming

_____ Normal   _____ Disheveled   _____ Unusual (explain): _____

_____

Hygiene

_____ Normal   _____ Body Odor   _____ Bad Breath

_____ Other (explain): _____

_____

Interpersonal Style

_____ Separates Comfortably From Parents (Child)

_____ Separates Easily From Parents   _____ Would Not Separate at All

_____ Appropriate, Cooperative   _____ Domineering, Demanding

_____ Provocative   _____ Guarded

_____ Submissive, Passive   _____ Threatening, Hostile, Aggressive

_____ Pouty   _____ Manipulative

_____ Impulsive   _____ Fearful

_____ Apathetic/Withdrawn   _____ Silly

_____ Destructive   _____ Dependent

_____ Crying   _____ Preoccupied

_____ Ambivalent   _____ Competitive

_____ Self-Destructive   _____ Other _____

                                        _____

Eye Contact

_____ Unremarkable   _____ Maintains Eye Contact

_____ Avoids Eye Contact   _____ Stares Into Space

_____ Other (explain): _____

_____

Speech

_____ Normal   _____ Pressured   _____ Slow

_____ Whiny   _____ Overly Loud   _____ Stutters

_____ Babyish   _____ Monotone   _____ Rambling

_____ Mute   _____ Impaired   _____ Broken

_____ Incoherent _____ Other _____

II. Behavioral/Affective/Psychomotor Functioning

Motor Activity

_____ Appropriate _____ Relaxed _____ Slow, Underactive

_____ Sedate _____ Psychomotor Retardation _____ Restless

_____ Pacing _____ Hyperactive _____ Mannerisms

_____ Tremors _____ Tics _____ Poor Coordination

_____ Other (explain): _____

Impulse Control

_____ Good _____ Fair _____ Poor

Mood

_____ Normal/Appropriate _____ Elated

_____ Optimistic, Cheerful _____ Pessimistic

_____ Guilty _____ Depressed

_____ Anxious _____ Angry

_____ Suspicious _____ Other (explain): _____

_____

Affect

_____ Appropriate _____ Inappropriate _____ Blunted, Flat

_____ Labile _____ Constricted _____ Other (explain):

_____

III. Cognitive Processes

Attention

_____ Normal _____ Distractible _____ Hypervigilant

Insight

_____ Fair to Good

_____ Limited; Difficulty Acknowledging Problems

_____ Absent; Denies Problems

_____ Blames Others for Problems

_____ Other (explain): _____

Memory

_____ Intact _____ Impaired

Thought Processes/Content

_____ Unremarkable _____ Flight of Ideas

_____ Blocking _____ Loose Associations

_____ Tangential, Circumstantial _____ Obsessive

_____ Delusion

Judgment

_____ Good _____ Fair to Good _____ Poor; Limited

_____ Significantly Impaired

IV. Intellectual Ability
Overall Intellectual Level

_____ Below Average _____ Average _____ Above Average

_____ Superior _____ Cannot Determine

_____ Other (explain): _____

Family History *(construct and attach genogram if appropriate)*

DSM-IV Multiaxial Diagnosis

	Diagnosis	Code Number	Diagnosis	Code Number
Axis I				
Axis II				
Axis III				
Axis IV				
Axis V	Current: _____	Highest in Last Year: _____		

Initial Core Issue Assessment:

Counselor's Conceptualization of the Client:

Counselor and Client Goals for Counseling:

Initial Counseling Plan: *(use additional sheets as necessary)*

chapter 4

designing counseling interventions: framing the child's living story

Once the assessment is complete, the next step is to construct and implement a counseling intervention plan. In the chapters that follow we address the different modalities (play therapy, expressive therapies, etc.) from which counselors may work. This chapter provides an overview of how counselors can broadly conceptualize the overall fit of the core issues approach when working within a child's world.

An effective counseling plan addresses the child's problem in a manner conceptually consistent with how that problem exists within the context of the child's life. In other words, the work in which the counselor engages the child should be consistent with the overall understanding of the problem and the goals of counseling (Horvath & Greenberg, 1987). Consider for a moment the nature of a core issues conceptualization. When a child is experiencing problems in life, there is consistency in the manner in which that child responds to those problems. Therefore, a child's problem can be examined within the context of broader thematic expressions of one or more core issues. Furthermore, these themes tend to emerge when the child is confronted with specific trigger situations. Because these response themes reflect the dynamic elements of a child's core issues, they can also serve as a frame for understanding a particular type of living story about the problematic nature of the child's current struggle. Consider once again the case of Monica presented in Chapter 3. Recall that at 6 years old Monica has already had many unpleasant and some traumatic experiences. Monica's struggle is a good example of just one of the many ways in which children can express their personal stories. As addressed in Chapter 3, using a core issues approach requires that the counselor start with a focus on accessing and understanding the nature of the child's story as a means of more specifically focusing the clinical intervention to be used. Focusing on the child's story is important because it increases the counselor's ability to assist in allowing children's stories to emerge, be recognized, and be validated. In this chapter, through the case study of Monica, we explore how a child's living story can be the cornerstone of the counseling process.

Client Core Issues Expressed as a Living Story

Effective counseling plans with children typically address the child's problem in a manner that is conceptually consistent with how that problem is viewed by adult stakeholders while simultaneously regarding the perspective of the child. Regardless of the age of the client, the work in which the counselor and client engage should be consistent with the overall understanding of the problem and the mutually agreed-upon goal of counseling (Horvath & Greenberg, 1987).

Let's revisit the nature of a core issues conceptualization. In Chapter 2, core issues were defined as the primary problematic elements of an individual's intrapersonal and interpersonal meaning-making system that, when activated, generate problematic responses to situational conditions over time. The implication is that when individuals respond to intrapersonal and interpersonal problems, they do so in a consistent manner. In accepting this definition, a clinician would have to consider the overall themes of a client's story, which are typically illuminated in relation to specific triggers. These response themes are characteristic of the client's core issues and therefore can allow for a conceptualization of the bigger picture of the client's perceptual experience.

Consider again the initial work done with Monica. In their first encounter, Monica communicates a problem to her counselor. Through her ball play, Monica communicates that she is unsure about relationships with others. She wants to feel powerful but creates interactions that others may experience as aggressive or manipulative. Monica's response to this problem, as described by her foster care parents, school personnel, and caseworker, includes feeling angry, being unable to stay on task, having sleep disturbances, and worrying her sister will be harmed. Forming a working diagnosis for Monica seems relatively simple. Even with the limited amount of information presented, a counselor might think in terms of one or more Axis I disorders, including adjustment disorder, attention deficit disorder, and/or separation anxiety. The key to appreciating Monica's core issue lies not within the details of the symptoms presented by the adults in her life but rather within the context of a living story that shows how Monica understands her world, how she responds when her core issues are triggered, and what aspects of her history have led her to behave in a maladaptive manner.

Remember that what the client communicates as "the problem" and the way in which he or she responds to the problem is of paramount importance. It is crucial to remember that the client's response to the problem can be as problematic as the problem itself; in Monica's case, her response of aggressive and self-injurious behavior can be even *more* problematic. It is for this reason that the counselor needs to have a clear understanding of what the child sees as the problem. Monica's view of the problem may be very different from that of the many adults in her life. Also know that what can be directly observed (typically behaviorally) or indirectly inferred (usually through an adult-centric lens) as the client's response to the problem may vary significantly from what the child knows or thinks to be true.

Children will not typically report a problem in the context of counseling. In most cases, it is the adult stakeholders who report the problem based on their own understanding. It is rarely difficult to make a distinction between the reported problem and the child's perception of the problem. In addition, it is also fairly simple to distinguish between the reported or perceived problem and the child's response to the problem. Children are typically quite good at communicating (i.e., through play and other behavioral manifestations) the difficult situations or uncomfortable feelings that have motivated their adult stakeholders to seek out counseling services on their behalf. The child's response to the problem can, in most cases, also be easily accessed. A child will usually communicate this information directly or indirectly to the counselor through play, behavior, or verbal communication. By using developmentally appropriate basic listening and therapy skills, the counselor will be able to help the child clarify the specific manner in which he or she has attempted to deal with the problem. As discussed in earlier chapters, assessing a client's core issues is different from making a traditional multiaxial diagnosis according to the *Diagnostic and Statistical Manual of Mental Disorders*. The core issues assessment creates a framework for uncovering the child's problem and in so doing allows the client's living story of intrapersonal and/or interpersonal relationships to unfold.

Constructivists, Living Stories, and Core Issues

What we refer to as the *living story* is the child's life narrative to date. It includes the repetitive reenactments of personal truths that are articulated through relational exchanges over time. The living story reflects the relational worldview of self, others, and the nature of personal beliefs about the world. In this sense, the living story is actually an expression of one's model of a personal relational reality. Therefore, a child's living story is the tale of how he or she goes about endeavoring to satisfy his or her perceived needs and wishes. It is the phenomenological perspective that dictates the child's personal living story. The child's story, therefore, can provide the counselor with a model of how the child makes sense of the world and responds to it.

Children are not born with their respective living stories. In general, children's narratives are authored by those within their relational sphere. Adults usually have a major influence on authoring narratives for young people because of the power and status they hold over children. When the adult author is also a professional (e.g., teacher), the living story that has been created for the child is more credible (Mullen, 2003). Children experience these other authored narratives as their own and hence live out the constructed truths inherent within them. Children construct their living stories through a process of interactions from which they draw conclusions about their selves, others, and the nature of the world. In order to access children's living stories, adults must recognize the culture of childhood and view the stories through a lens that honors that culture. In addition, children's living stories can be less ingrained than those of their adult counterparts solely because of the solidification of living stories that takes place over time and as a result of the repetitive reenactments of relational experiences. Kegan (1982) argued that people (including children) are constantly engaged in a process of observing the world and then cognitively constructing an organized meaningful whole of those observations. This act of making meaning is a continuous procedure and a primary trademark of what it is to be human. Perry (1970) stated this clearly and concisely: "What organisms do is organize and what human organisms do is organize meaning" (p. 3).

From a postmodern-constructivist perspective, the acts of observing, assessing, and organizing meaning result in the creation of a phenomeno-logical reality. A personally created reality can be understood as a "truth" that serves as the template for how an individual perceives and responds to the environment (Babrow, Kline, & Rawlins, 2005; Parry & Doan, 1994; Ramsay, 1998). We place quotation marks around "truth" to stress the constructivists' assertion that there are limits to any form of objective knowing derived from one's meaning-making process (Spence, 2003). When an individual constructs truths that are maladaptive, then prob-lematic thoughts, feelings, and behaviors can result. When the individual responds to the world from a set of maladaptive truths, his or her ability to cope and achieve desired goals and outcomes becomes compromised.

Each child's personal truths provide the counselor with both an exigent barrier to the consideration of alternative ways of understanding and a privileged advantage. It is important to recognize that personal "truths" are not easily relinquished. Counselors are challenged when children hold on to personal truths based on a core issue maladaptive schema that have nevertheless allowed them to make sense and meaning of self, others, and the world. How each child functions intrapersonally and interpersonally is based in the truth that he or she has constructed. Al-though children's chronological history is not as extensive as that of their adult counterparts, it is equally as important from a phenomenological perspective. Although children have not had as much time to create and use their personal truths, these personal truths are still the frameworks from which they operate relationally in the world. Furthermore, by their very nature personal truths are usually limited by the child's capacity to engage in perspective taking. Children, quite understandably, construct limited truths because of their concrete cognitive operations, which are the hallmark of early developmental stages. All personal truths, includ-ing those of children, serve to create a comfortable state of homeostasis. Homeostasis is often cherished by clients because change is uncomfortable and in many cases no other reality or truth is available. Even when patterns of behavior lead to undesirable outcomes, clients are reluctant to let go of a constructed truth. The idea that change may ultimately lead to growth and healing holds little sway because a client has no reference point for conceiving a new way of being. It is for this reason that counselors must observe clients' unique kind of devotion to their constructed truths without disrespecting or pathologizing that world. This characteristic of the self creates a set of clinical challenges for counselors when it comes to designing a treatment plan.

Yet this challenge can also be viewed through the constructivist lens as an advantage. Because "truth" is a personal and subjective construction, it can also be personally deconstructed. This deconstruction involves examining each component objectively, preparing it to be reconstructed in the context of counseling such that the reconstructed truth is adaptive and more consistent with both current environmental demands as well as the client's needs and desires. Therefore, if the counselor can demonstrate to the client an understanding of the thoughts, feelings, and behaviors associated with the client's maladaptive story, he or she can help the client see that there may be the possibility of alternative stories. Narrative approaches to counseling focus on examining the multiple and complex elements embedded in a client's story. This examination provides an opportunity to illuminate the nature of the problem for both the client and the counselor. Unearthing the client's narrative thus provides a foundation for designing interventions specifically for the individual client and the core issues with which the client struggles.

Core Issues and Living Story Narratives

Even if they cannot articulate it verbally, all children have a story that (a) reflects important events that have left salient impressions and (b) has helped them establish truths about the self, others, and the nature of the world and their place in it. It is through these stories that children formulate their meaning-making systems. As children express their personal narratives, the most salient aspects of their lives become apparent. This often includes the painful aspects of life with which a child attempts to cope.

We propose that by paying attention to core issues narratives, counselors can look deeper into the lives of children to discover the basis for their problematic thoughts, feelings, and behavior. Counselors must have the vision to see past the unauthorized narratives advanced by those who play controlling roles in children's lives. They must have the unique ability to look beyond behavioral manifestations and pathologizing contexts when conceptualizing children's struggles. However, assisting children in communicating the whole story and listening for the key elements that signify the core struggle is no easy task (Parry & Doan, 1994; Spence, 2003). It is complicated by children's developmental inclination to communicate by showing or doing rather than verbalizing. Children often tell their stories through play as well as other expressive modalities. Although an arduous task, helping children with respect to their core issues is crucial. Wanner (1994) argued that the goal of the helping professional should be for clients to integrate and synthesize so that they feel whole. This is the basic goal of designing interventions that are aimed at addressing core issues.

Children's Narratives and Culture

Culture is always a component of the meaning-making process. It influences the ways in which children understand themselves, others, and the larger world. The plural term *cultures* is used to express the broad and overlapping nature of cultural influence on one's life (e.g., family heritage, gender, community, religion, sexual orientation, levels of socioeconomic advantage, physical ability, ethnicity, race, geographic region; Halstead, 2007). When assessing core issues with children, counselors must be aware of the multiple cultural influences, including relevant subcultures, at play in children's meaning-making processes. Culture is always reflected in personal narratives (Halliday, 1989; Hardy, 1977; Howard, 1991; McHale, 1992; Nussbaum, 1988; Polkinghorne, 1988; Wanner, 1994; Witherell & Noddings, 1991).

The family is the child's first cultural influence. It is within the family that children begin to construct narratives that reflect the relational worlds in which they must live and determine how to survive. The primary task of all children is to survive, regardless of how functional or dysfunctional the home environment is at any point in time. For this reason, children's stories always present themes that describe what they believed they needed to do in order to survive. In addition, during the early phases of childhood, children are dualistic thinkers. Their all-or-nothing perspective of self, others, and the nature of the world leaves few gray areas for consideration. They cannot cognitively engage in a process that would allow them to think in more complex ways. Yet regardless of their limited development and cognition, children experience their living stories as narrative truth. These early survival stories are the building blocks of meaning and are rarely deconstructed for the sake of testing their validity. The perception of the survival story is in fact the child's reality. Parry and Doan (1994) captured the essence of this phenomenon:

> If the stories into which children are born, create and shape their emotions, they do so by constructing what the children *believe* to be real . . . The more, however, their very survival seems to be threatened . . . the more rigidly incorporated such stories become. When a child's world-shaping stories come to imply risks to his/her survival, they include two significant messages: "This is what you must avoid to survive" (either physically or psychologically) and "This is what you can do to survive—and maybe even be loved." (p. 38, italics in the original)

In Chapter 2 we discussed how it is imperative to understand that children can operate only from their basic emotional or core needs. These needs, which expand over the course of one's development, are the building blocks of children's living stories. Each living story begins with the child needing to know that he or she will be cared for. That need is quickly integrated into a living story that details what is necessary for the child to feel safe, loved, and protected. Parry and Doan (1994) suggested that the normal socialization process uses the need for love and caring to gain leverage over the child, who otherwise would not likely conform to social mores. This process involves setting conditions for the child in the form of an "if/then" statement: "If only you will do _____, then I (we) will love you." As discussed earlier, children are concrete in terms of their cognitive processing and thus operate as dualistic thinkers. Thus, it is easy to see how children would accept this if/then message. They have little power over the environment; they recognize their power status; and they simultaneously are in great need of love, nurturance, and protection.

As discussed in Chapter 2, Young et al. (2003) identified 18 core issue schemas organized under five individually specific core issue domains. Each of the core issue domains relates to a specific core emotional need that, in one way or another, has not been adequately met. These unmet core needs are the basis for understanding the core issues narrative or the client's problematic living story. Any core emotional need that was repeatedly not met is likely to become a salient and steadfast theme in the client's living story. It is important to note again that when working with children, the unmet needs that serve as the catalyst for the development of core issues are usually ongoing. Although assessing core issues in children is complicated by the fact that they do not have the same intensity and unwavering characteristics as those in adults, they are also more readily confronted and altered.

As noted in Chapter 3, there are 18 core issues, each with three different coping adaptations (i.e., compensation, avoidance, and surrender). The following discussion illuminates how the counselor can draw from these core issues and coping styles to establish a framework for using the child's personal narrative.

Core Issue Case Analysis and Narrative Themes in the Living Story

Every client provides the counselor with an opportunity to cull through all sorts of information. The skilled clinician engages in a process that focuses systematically on those aspects of information that will, when taken together, provide the clearest understanding of the client and the issues with which the client is dealing. Again, Monica's case serves as a good illustration.

Monica and her sister lived with her mother, older half-brother, and mother's paramour. As a toddler, Monica spent most of her time in the care of her maternal grandmother, who initially was very nurturing and affectionate but then became less so when she was reprimanded by Monica's mother for "spoiling" Monica. Monica was 18 months old when her sister was born, and her grandmother cared for both girls during the day while

Monica's mother worked. However, these days turned into late evenings as her mother increasingly socialized with her friends. Monica often cried and threw tantrums when her mother dropped her off at her grandmother's house and also when she was picked up and brought back home. Monica would reportedly tantrum with such intensity that she would often soil herself in the process. Although Monica was in her mother's care, she and her sister would be left alone for hours when her mother would go out on weekends. As these tantrums became increasingly frequent, Monica's mother finally reached out for help after being investigated for neglect and child abuse. She participated in several home-based parenting and support programs. Despite these supports, Monica's mother began to use severe physical means in an effort to discipline her. During this time she became more involved in using marijuana, crack cocaine, and alcohol. To make matters worse, Monica's maternal grandmother and caregiver died unexpectedly. Monica's mother quit her job to care for her two young daughters. However, the court declared that she was unable to care for them, and they were subsequently placed in foster care.

The key components of Monica's story presented in Chapter 3 will enable the counselor to make preliminary hypotheses regarding what sort of core issue(s) might be central to Monica's life. With the additional information provided here, the initial assessment gains validity. The loss of her grandmother and the emotional absence of both biological parents coupled with the experiences of abuse and neglect during Monica's toddlerhood would indicate the core issue domain of Disconnection and Rejection and, within that domain, the possible core issues of abandonment/instability, mistrust/abuse, and emotional deprivation—nurturance type.

The next step in the assessment process is for the counselor to determine how the client responds when this particular core issue gets triggered. In so doing the counselor comes to better understand the client's story and relate it to the client's core issues. In an effort to keep this example as simple and clear as possible, we address only the core issue of abandonment/instability here.

Remember that Monica may use three separate coping mechanisms in her attempts to deal with the core issue of abandonment/instability. Each coping mechanism would manifest differently as a distinct narrative theme. Monica's response to the core issue of abandonment/instability using a compensation coping style would be indicated by her neediness. Or it may involve Monica maintaining close physical proximity to the counselor during the session and being reluctant to leave at the end of the session. Personal space is a function of development and one that can also be viewed through the lens of the culture of childhood. Compared to members of the dominant U.S. culture, especially adults, children tend to place themselves in closer proximity to others. For a needy child, being in close proximity to others can be very comforting. If Monica were to use an avoidance adaptation coping strategy, she would make efforts not to engage in relationships for fear that she would be abandoned again. This would be especially evident if the counselor used, for example, a child-centered counseling approach. Monica's use of an avoidance coping strategy may be indicated by her refusal to enter the playroom or to make eye contact with the therapist. She might also test limits by acting in ways that may be interpreted as a form of dualistic expression (e.g., "What if I do this? Will you leave me then?"). Finally, if Monica were to use a surrender adaptation coping style, the counselor could anticipate that Monica would attempt to form relationships with the very people who would be most likely to be emotionally distant with or dismissive of her. Through such interactions with others, Monica would confirm her belief that people will continue to abandon her.

Once the counselor has a working hypothesis of the client's core issue, the next step is analyzing the client's coping adaptation and response style. For example, the counselor clarifies Monica's coping adaptation by observing her response style as she demonstrates her strategies through play and other activities. Counselors who use a core issues case conceptualization can gain a clearer understanding of what motivates individual clients to respond to core issues. It is this understanding that aids counselors in their ability to empathize with clients to appreciate their phenomenological perspective. This is why thinking through the child's narrative is so critical to conducting efficacious clinical work. Refer back to Table 3 in Chapter 3. This table highlights all of the possible core issues and the three alternative coping responses that can accompany each.

Temporal Elements and Core Issues Stories

The counselor needs to listen to the content of the child's narrative and how the child's various modalities are used to express that narrative. The counselor may want to contemplate what the child is trying to communicate through his or her interactions and play. The time-linked stories that a client relates either have taken place in the past, are taking place in the present, or will take place in the future (Ricoeur, 1984). The counselor can make sense of the temporal element of a client's stories by recognizing that stories from the past provide a historical perspective of the client's experiences. Stories that are communicated about the present demonstrate the current struggle the client is experiencing. Stories set in the future convey the client's hopes and fears about what lies ahead. Considering these three temporal elements, the three coping adaptation responses, and the three self-in-relation elements is a very useful way of conceptualizing the client. Figure 7 graphically depicts a model for making sense of the varied stories clients communicate in and across sessions. This model simplifies the core issues framework by providing a means for evaluating the larger narrative presented in a series of stories about self, others, or the world across a personal timeline.

Designing and Implementing the Counseling Intervention

Once the counselor has formed an assessment of the client's core issue struggles and the client's living story, an individualized counseling in-

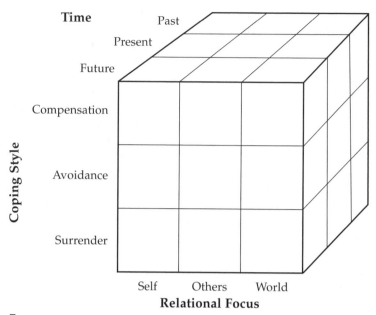

Figure 7

A Model for Analyzing the Living Story

tervention plan can be designed and implemented. Remember that it is not our intention to provide a comprehensive primer on child-focused therapies. Rather, we include this section to demonstrate the core issues approach from start to finish as it is used with children. What follows is one of many possible interventions. This particular example describes play therapy; other types of child-focused therapies are explained in the chapters that follow.

We recognize both the complexity and intuitiveness of our thesis. Simply put, this thesis maintains that individuals live by personal truths that they have constructed about themselves, others, and the world. These truths organize the ways in which these individuals deal with the greater and lesser struggles with which they are confronted and thus eventually compose their individual personal narratives. It is through these narratives that individuals construct and maintain their relational reality. An initial set of personal truths is constructed during childhood in an environment over which the child has little control (Halstead, 2007; Mullen, 2003). When challenges arise during childhood, the child uses these truths as a way of understanding self, others, and the world and attempts to resolve those challenges based on this personal reality. Personal truths and living stories change over time as they become outdated, as they become insufficient for ordering one's worldview, and as individuals gain the inherent power and status that comes with maturity. Truths created in childhood are strongly anchored to an individual's personal narratives and thus often become the source of problems rather than the effective coping strategy they once were. If the counselor accepts this thesis as a usable conceptual framework for understanding the nature of a client's problems, then it seems reasonable that the goal of any counseling intervention would need to be to address the client's personally constructed truths about self, others, and world.

Counselors who use the client's core issues as a living story framework have four process goals when designing and implementing a counseling intervention. The first goal is to help the child understand the core issues and to provide an opportunity to communicate the nature of the core issues in a way that is consistent with the child's developmental stage. The second goal is to help the child gain insight into how the core issues impact his or her experiences with self, others, and the world and how maintaining this personal living story will result in ongoing problems. These first two goals are most usually accomplished through conducting a core issues assessment that includes discussion with the stakeholders in the child's life, providing the child an opportunity to share his or her story verbally and allowing the child to communicate through the natural medium of play. Children in child-centered counseling will gain insight into their own thoughts, feelings, and behaviors as well as be able to problem solve, act prosocially, and experiment with various aspects of self (Landreth, 2002b). The third process goal involved in designing and implementing a counseling intervention is to deconstruct the living story. This can also occur in the context of child-centered counseling as children are given the freedom to pull apart the various elements of the core issues story as it currently exists, question its subjective truths, and experiment with alternative truths. Once the counselor has provided an environment that allows the child to deconstruct the living story, the fourth goal is to provide the opportunity for the child to choose a prosocial and relationship-enhancing path that permits him or her to construct a more adaptive story that reflects the types of outcomes the child desires.

This process involves helping the child author a story that reflects his or her current prosocial and relational needs and wishes. The counselor helps the child create a worldview that consists of more adaptive thoughts, feelings, and behavioral responses than the one currently in place. The third and fourth goals of this process are at the heart of the counseling/play therapy intervention and are addressed in detail in the next section.

Deconstructing and Reconstructing the Client's Living Story

Parry and Doan (1994) asserted that the process of story deconstruction and reconstruction consists of several steps that help the client become more adaptive in life. These steps, which are also elements of the counseling process, are as follows:

1. Identify the current childhood survival story.
2. Support the child for using coping strategies that have allowed him or her to survive.

3. Connect the common aspects of the multiple working drafts of the core issues stories and clarify the assumptive truths that have been constructed about the self, others, and the nature of the world.
4. Externalize the story so that it is located outside of the self.
5. Identify the core issue triggers and how those issues are often the catalyst for strong feelings, thoughts, and behaviors.
6. Identify the limitations of the child's current less adaptive story.
7. Provide the child with a therapeutic and relational environment that allows him or her to discover and use various ways and means to stop responding to the old story.
8. Work toward helping the child create and implement a new alternative story. (Halstead, 2007; Parry & Doan, 1994)

Conceptualizing within this framework involves working systematically through each step of this process.

Task 1:
Identify the Current Childhood Survival Story

During childhood, children begin the process of constructing subjective truths about themselves, others, and the nature of the world. Children do this by constantly evaluating the environment and making meaning from these experiences in an effort to figure out how to best interact with the world and simply survive. Children's survival stories in progress, then, are embedded in their historical and current unmet needs as well as their desires.

In the beginning phase of the counseling process, the counselor needs to identify the big picture themes in the child's story. One should not expect that the child will directly state his or her core issue themes. Rather, the child's communication of themes manifests verbally, nonverbally, and through play. It is also important that the counselor communicate accurate empathy when addressing the child's core issue or story themes. This is most commonly accomplished through engaging in reflective listening responses. Acknowledging and honoring these themes will allow the child to feel understood. When the reflections of feeling responses encompass the big picture of the core issue, the story is illuminated to the child. White (1986) defined this crucial step in the counseling process as defining the specifications of personhood. This step encompasses the roadblocks individuals encounter when faced with challenges.

To this point, we have focused the discussion on the child's emerging childhood survival story. Children do not create these stories without context. Each child's family is part of the larger story, and because it is the primary culture of children it typically plays a prominent role (Mullen, 2003). Regular consultation and collaboration with family is therefore recommended for counselors using a core issues framework so that the influence of larger family stories can be understood and evaluated. The counselor's knowledge of the family story places the child's story in an important context. The counselor can then respond to the child's individual story with the added richness of a contextual view.

Task 2:
Support the Child for Using Coping Strategies That Have Allowed Him or Her to Survive

In child-centered counseling, the child is accepted exactly how he or she is (Axline, 1969; Landreth, 2002b) despite maladaptive thoughts, feelings, and behaviors that are consistent with his or her existing personal story. The counselor understands that the child holds onto this story tightly for two reasons. First, this story is the basis for the child's safety and security. Second, an alternative narrative that the child can believe in has not presented itself. Personal truths, even those in young children that do not have a great deal of relational history tied to them, are not given up easily. Children are usually involved in counseling interventions because of their maladaptive behavior. Counselors who philosophically respect and honor children view these maladaptive behaviors through a lens of coping. In order to provide these children with an alternative story, counselors operate from a place of acceptance and respect so that the children can explore more prosocial and adaptive story themes. Maintaining this humanistic lens enhances the speedy building of rapport. Children are sometimes confused when they experience empathy from one who understands and accepts their living narrative. One of us, after making an accurate empathic response, once had a child ask, "How do you know how to read my mind?"

Task 3:
Connect the Common Aspects of the Core Issues Story and Clarify the Assumptive Truths That Have Been Constructed About the Self, Others, and the Nature of the World

As the relationship with the child progresses, the counselor listens and watches for the various elements of the core issues stories that emerge. Often this process starts at intake when parents or caregivers report the problems the child is currently displaying. The counselor needs to recognize the difference between the story authored by the child and the story authored by an adult caregiver. In keeping with the philosophy of client-centered counseling, the child's story is the one that must be accepted. Assessing the stories of stakeholders as well as the stories the child tells and plays out for common elements (i.e., unmet core needs; coping style; trigger situations; resulting thoughts, feelings, and behaviors) will help to clarify the assumptive truths that have been constructed about the self, others, and the nature of the world.

Task 4:
Externalize the Story so That It Is Located Outside of the Self

Children tend instinctively to engage in play as a way of experimenting. Through play, children place personal experiences outside of themselves so that their stories can be experimented with, altered, contemplated, and challenged. Many children in child-centered counseling use self-directed role play to experiment with a variety of ways of thinking, feeling, and behaving. They engage in the process of viewing the story that they have lived and are living from a position located outside the self. They can then (within the confines of their development) gain perspective on what is and has been problematic. (Sandplay therapy can also be used in this way with children.) Once the "problematic story" is located outside of the child, the child can examine himself or herself without the defenses and developmental limitations that stand in the way in verbal-based counseling.

Locating the "problem" outside of the child is also important when collaborating and consulting with stakeholders in the child's life. Popular culture and the mental health industry alike reinforce negative "personal truths" with the *Diagnostic and Statistical Manual of Mental Disorders* system of diagnostic labeling. For example, when counselors say with regard to a student, "She is on the spectrum" or "He is attention-deficit/hyperactive," they are using the diagnosis beyond merely labeling as a means of identifying the child as the disorder. Parents and other stakeholders are not working in their own best interest or in the best interest of the child when they label the child as "being" depressed, oppositional, anxious, bulimic, bipolar, angry, or any one of the other many labels that get attached to the child's struggle. A diagnostic category can interfere with and even close down opportunities for further exploration, especially when the child is aware of it. For example, one child immediately stated to one of us, "I am oppositional defiant disorder" during our very first session.

It behooves counselors to help not only the child but also the stakeholders in the child's life to view the problem through a lens that does not label the child as that problem. This perspective indicates that the problem needs to be remedied, but the child does not need to be "fixed" in order to be "okay" or of value. This is best conveyed by giving the problematic aspects of the child's behavior (e.g., anger) a name that then can be referenced in the third person: "So when Mr. Anger comes to visit, what does it feel like?" "What can we do to keep Mr. Anger from coming to your house so often?" By externalizing the problem in this way, the child, counselor, and parents can join together as a team to oppose anger rather than identify the problem as one of an angry child (Parry & Doan, 1994).

Task 5:
Identify the Core Issue Triggers and How Those Issues Are Often the Catalyst for Strong Feelings, Thoughts, and Behaviors

Counselors can anticipate that the core issue problems are obfuscated. They can also anticipate that the thoughts, feelings, and behaviors associated with a particular core issue will present themselves as the issue gets triggered in specific situational conditions. Consequently, it is helpful to the child, and to those closely connected to the child, to identify the child's trigger points. This serves to bring forth the awareness needed for the child to understand what pushes his or her buttons. Adults and even siblings may be helpful in identifying a child's trigger points. A child's caregivers will be more helpful if they learn to understand and communicate about a child's responses through a core issues framework rather than a pathology view.

Parents and other stakeholders can be encouraged to keep a simple journal that documents situational conditions in which the child seems to use the maladaptive behaviors, thoughts, and expressions of feelings as they relate to the theme of the core issue. The journal entries could include the events leading up to a problematic episode; the thoughts, feelings, and behaviors that are triggered by the episode; the client's response to the triggered experience; and the consequences of the event (Halstead, 2007).

Task 6:
Identify the Limitations of the Child's Current Less Adaptive Story

Consider the child's draft of the childhood survivor story as he or she is in the midst of creating it or has recently constructed it. Also, consider how the story may address the core issue. The counselor must look at how the components of this story (i.e., core issues and coping adaptation) are getting in the child's way. An overview of the client's history, collaboration and consultation with stakeholders, and reconnecting to the reason for the initial referral or presenting problem are all means of determining what is getting in the child's way of engaging the relational environment in more adaptive ways.

Task 7:
Provide the Child With a Therapeutic and Relational Environment That Allows Him or Her to Discover and Use Various Ways and Means to Stop Responding to the Old Story

This task is a difficult challenge for the child. Change does not come easily, even to children. Adults may sometimes dismiss or minimize how children are impacted by change. Remember that children are in the process of creating and solidifying a set of personal truths that make it possible for them to understand how life works. Adhering to internal guidelines about how life works allows children to feel more settled. Therefore, giving up a personal truth is always met with some level of resistance. When the alternative truth is experienced as being of better quality than the old truth, the overall process of change is less arduous.

The tenets of the child-centered counseling philosophy and approach (Axline, 1969; Landreth, 2002b) support the counselor and child in taking on this task. The most salient aspect of a child-centered counseling intervention is creating a relationship with the child within which the child feels free to express the self and to try on different versions of the self (Axline, 1969). This philosophy also suggests that children have two paths from which to choose. They can be either prosocial or antisocial. Children will choose the antisocial path when they do not have relational experiences that provide the opportunity to travel down the prosocial path. One of the ways to help children make changes is to provide space for them to lead the way in the relationship with the play therapist. In leading, children begin to make decisions about themselves and deal with the natural consequences that occur. They get to try on various aspects of who they are, essentially playing out different personal storylines. Therefore, in this phase of counseling children can begin to revise current stories and are empowered to author their own story.

Child-centered counseling is a gradual process (Axline, 1969), and understandably this component of the process takes time. It behooves the counselor to recognize (and communicate to invested adults in the lives of the child) the strength with which all individuals hold on to personal truths and to realize that the amount of time it takes children to make changes is linked to their experiences of control and power both inside and outside of counseling.

Task 8:
Work Toward Helping the Child Create and Implement a New Alternative Story

Over the course of the intervention the child gains insight into his or her survival story and the way in which that story causes problems that lead to discomfort and stress. For many children these problems are experienced as not being liked or always getting into trouble. The final counseling task, from a core issues approach, is to help the client create a new and more adaptive story that allows for better relationships with self, others, and the world. During this process, the play therapist acts as coauthor, editor, and publisher as the child tries out his or her new and more adaptive story role. Many children need the status of the play therapist as an adult and his or her credibility as a professional for their new story to be heard and accepted by other adults (Mullen, 2003).

Counselors who work with children are prepared through their professional education programs to assess their clients through a diagnostic lens. Doing so serves to generate treatment protocol based on a symptom reduction approach that is tied to pathological and abnormal constructions of what and how children present. However, viewing a child from a core issues perspective allows for a deeper and richer understanding of the child's relational worldview that generated his or her symptoms in the first place. For example, one of us has had clients' parents make statements such as "Good luck when he [their own 5-year-old] comes in here. He'll probably bite you; he's a monster!" or "My kid [an 8-year-old girl] is so strange; that's why she has no friends." Such comments, and the beliefs that underlie them, dominate the worldviews of some adults who are not able to tap the worldviews of children who are often only responding the best way they know how. The counselor who focuses solely on the dominant story misses opportunities to discover the evidence that can support and nurture an alternative story. For instance, the child referred to as a "monster" by his parents often used "please" and "thank you" in responding to his counselor. These prosocial exchanges offered important evidence that a kind and willing child lived within the dominant "monster" story. The goal is to help the child recognize and develop this alternative and more adaptive story. Work toward this goal begins the moment a counselor believes an alternative story can exist and is open to the evidence that supports it. Often the counselor's hope can be communicated to the child through acceptance, which is the cornerstone of a core issues approach. This is similar to the philosophy of child-centered counseling (Axline, 1969; Landreth, 2002b). Although this idea may sound simplistic, it presents a significant clinical challenge, because the child's initial presentation can drown out any information that is inconsistent with his or her relational view of the world. A core issues approach to designing an intervention can be an incredibly powerful asset in meeting the challenge of working with deeply troubled children.

Summary

This chapter provides a framework for the intervention phases that are elemental to the counseling process. This process starts with the counselor helping the child recognize an emerging childhood survival story and how that story is tied to the core problematic issues that continue to plague the child in a variety of situations. Of course, this is communicated to the child in a way that honors his or her development, cognitive level, and salient cultures. Childhood is recognized as a distinct culture by the counselor, who views the client through a cross-cultural lens. Viewing childhood in this manner, the counselor can support the child's response to childhood environments as a means of coping to survive. Developmentally appropriate interventions foster opportunities for both the counselor and the child to build rapport and to minimize the child's use of defense responses. Linking the themes of the various core issues stories and recognizing the supposed truths that have been created about the self, others, and the nature of the world permit the counselor to expand the child's story and better understand the nature of "the problem" as it has manifested over time. When that problem is examined from a perspective outside of the self, the assessment becomes focused on the problem, not the person. The counselor identifies the core issue triggers and how those issues fuel strong feelings, thoughts, and behaviors that in turn worsen the problem. Illuminating the limitations of the child's old and less adaptive story helps the child create change by experimenting with other ways of thinking, feeling, and behaving. Through this experimentation, first with the counselor and then outside of the context of counseling, the child establishes and chooses more adaptive options for responding to the core issue and transforming his or her relational worldview of self, others, and the world.

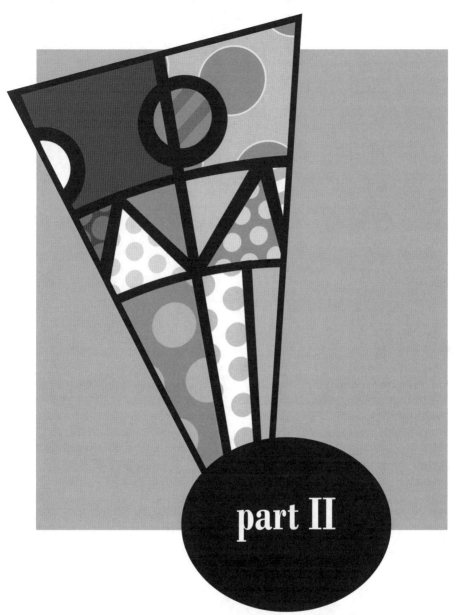

part II

Intervention Modalities and Children's Core Issues

establishing the therapeutic relationship

The emphasis on the preparation and training of professional counselors focuses on verbal-based strategies for use with adults (Mullen, 2003). To be effective at counseling children, counselors must do more than just adapt these skills. They must also focus on mastering specific skill sets consistent with the particular developmental level at which the child is functioning. Counselors of children also regularly consult with parents, educational professionals, and social services agencies; thus, consultation skills are a secondary, but crucial, skill set. Finally, child counselors also need to hold a particular philosophy that is consistent with the culture of childhood. This philosophy takes the form of a set of principles that helps to establish therapeutic connections and build a strong counseling relationship over time. This chapter provides a brief overview of the fundamental principles of counseling children. Most important are the various factors that allow counselors to connect with children by respecting their developmental stages and the childhood cultures that they reflect.

In this book we have chosen to focus on experiential and expressive modalities over other methods of working with children. When illustrating the core issues approach to working with children, we do not emphasize verbal-based approaches. This is not because we do not value what verbal-based approaches have to offer; rather, we recognize that most counselors are already familiar with and skilled at using these approaches. However, many practitioners have limited experience with using verbal and nonverbal interventions when counseling children. Here we offer some essential alternatives to verbal interventions. Our combined clinical, supervision, and teaching expertise has allowed us to develop case studies of interventions that are developmentally well-suited to helping children using a core issues approach. These interventions include play therapy, sandplay therapy, expressive arts in counseling, and narrative approaches to counseling. It is our belief that these case studies provide for a richer understanding of the core issues approach to counseling children. In the chapters that follow we provide a brief overview of these approaches to counseling children as a means of illustrating the core issues approach.

The Culture of Childhood

In order to build a strong counseling relationship, it is extremely important for the counselor to demonstrate a deep respect not only for children but for childhood itself through conceptualizing it as an important subculture. Holding this particular philosophical perspective and demonstrating it while working with children can be challenging. Children and their manner of thought are often dismissed by adults as being funny or incorrect. For example, when an adolescent or adult is described as being childish, this is considered an insult and indicates disrespect. When counseling children from a cross-cultural orientation, respect is critical. Demonstrating a desire to understand and respect another's worldview is an important keystone of the counseling relationship. Showing respect toward children requires counselors to do some things that would not be considered therapeutic, respectful, or even professional when working with adults. In working with children, counselors need to engage in a process of matching their interactions with the child's stage of development across the physical, emotional, and cognitive contact domains.

When counselors think about working with children within the physical domain, they need to consider differences in stature. Because child clients are usually much smaller than adult clients, the counselor needs to make adjustments to both the waiting area and the counseling room. The counselor also needs to consider his or her own physical posture when attending to a child. For example, it is respectful and culturally sensitive for a counselor to take a position that levels eye contact with the child. To maintain eye contact with children, use similarly sized seating or sit on the floor, if necessary. The counseling room and furniture should be child friendly, and seating should be comfortable and appropriately sized for children of all ages. There are additional benefits to making these accommodations. First, the counselor is better able to observe the child's facial expressions when at the same physical level as opposed to looking down at the child. Second, the counselor can hear the child more clearly, especially if the session is taking place in a classroom in which other children and adults are active. Third, by attempting to match size, the counselor appears to reduce, to some degree, the inherent power he or she possesses. Fourth, the child can see the counselor directly and this helps to avoid any distortions in nonverbal communications that come from having to look up at someone.

Within the affective domain, counselors need to make shifts in traditional approaches to counseling in order to engage children more effectively on an emotional level. In order for counselors to be able to demonstrate accurate empathic understanding with children, they have to take into consideration the important developmental hallmarks of childhood. Children, not unlike their adult counterparts, need to feel that they are being listened to and clearly understood. One way for the counselor to indicate to the child that he or she is listening is to paraphrase what the child has just said to demonstrate that the counselor is capturing and reflecting the child's total message. The typical use of paraphrasing with adult clients involves the counselor responding with the gist of what the client has said by using different words so that the counselor is not merely repeating or parroting the client's words. When the client is a child, some important communication is nonverbal and takes place through facial expressions, body language, play, artwork, and other expressive mediums. Hence, paraphrasing involves not only repeating words but mirroring what the child has communicated through all expressive modalities. Of course, this mirroring needs to be done in a subtle and positive way so that the child does not feel like the counselor is disrespectfully mimicking him or her.

Reflective responses can include the subtle mirroring of actions to demonstrate to the child that the counselor is capturing how the child feels. Children do not use a great many feeling words in their everyday speech. One reason for this is that, especially in the early years of childhood, emotions are not well differentiated. Another reason is that they have yet to develop a vocabulary of sufficient adjectives such that they can convert their affective experiences into the verbal and intellectual context of language. The communication experiences that children have with adults may play a role in their use of feeling words to describe their experiences. Adults tend to minimize or deny the emotional experiences of children (Mullen, 2007). That is, when children do state or communicate how they are feeling to adults, they are often given messages that they do not have those feelings or that they should not have those feelings. Adults often minimize children's feelings and experiences.

A few examples illustrate this point. Imagine that a child, Emily, announces to her teacher, "I hate my mother!" A typical adult would probably respond to the child by saying something like "You do not hate your mother" or "Don't say that; it's not nice." These examples show how the child clearly expressed how she was feeling but the adult's response communicated to the child that she did not feel hate or that she was wrong for how she felt. A child may say, "This is the worst day of my life." Think for a minute about how you might respond to such a statement, or how other adults have responded to similar statements from children. Many helping professionals have difficulty seeing a child in pain and often respond in a manner that seeks to minimize that pain. An example of minimizing the child's true feelings might be to say, "Oh come on now, it really isn't that bad." To the child, however, it really might be that bad. Thus, it is very important that when a child expresses emotional content, the counselor accepts it and validates the importance of that emotional reality. Examples of emotional minimization or dismissal in day-to-day interactions between children and adults are limitless. All one has to do is listen to the ways in which adults respond when children share how they feel. Sadly, too many adults demonstrate too little respect for the affective world in which children live.

In order to be effective listeners with children, counselors cannot deny or minimize children's feelings and experiences. Honoring and showing respect for what children share is crucial to the relationship-building process. In order to do this effectively, it is important to be able to meet children at their specific stage of development. That is, counselors must develop the capacity to suspend typical adult-to-adult communication and embrace appropriate interactions with children. They must be thoughtful about the congruence of their nonverbal and verbal communication. Children, especially those who come from relationally challenging environments, are expert readers of facial expressions and body language. Therefore, they become wary of people who say one thing and present another through their nonverbal communication. In addition, children have shorter attention spans than their adult counterparts. This means that responses to children in counseling need to be succinct. A relatively large portion of childhood is characterized by concrete cognitive processing (Piaget, 1969). Children who possess a worldview framed by concrete thinking may not always understand adultcentric verbalizations. Counselors have to assess the qualitative nature of a child's cognitive processes and then communicate in a manner that respects the child's cognitive developmental stage and style.

Finally, counselors need to use vocabulary and language that is child friendly and that is developmentally and culturally suited to the individual child. Counselors can take several steps to improve their facility for using language that is appropriate to children. For example, they must be familiar with popular culture references that children deem important. Watching television geared to preschool and primary school-age children is excellent preparation for better engaging children. Similarly, being familiar with technology and computer gaming systems can be important when it comes to interacting with children and their world. Being familiar with these references will allow counselors to speak, or at least understand, the language and concepts that children might relate to counseling. Children are also not impressed with vocabulary that is beyond their comprehension. "Big words" tend to lack meaning and alienate children. Therefore, counselors working with children need to assess their language use and watch for nonverbal and verbal cues that children do not understand.

Because children communicate using multiple modalities of expression, counselors should be flexible in reaching out to them. Children very often tell their stories best through play and art and express their feelings through relational interactions that include gestures and facial expressions. Some approaches for counseling children provide more structure than others, but all are responsive to the needs of children and promote their ability to be heard within the cultural context of childhood.

Summary

The first step in providing effective counseling services involves establishing and building upon a strong counseling relationship. Counseling children involves a set of challenges that include recognizing the cultural norms and mores within each of the developmental stages of childhood. The next chapters discuss the direct uses of narrative therapy, play therapy, sand tray therapy, and artwork when counseling children from a core issues perspective.

narratives and alternative stories for healing and enhancing autonomy

For many children, traditional talk therapies provide only partial therapeutic release, learning, and growth. This is particularly true for preadolescents (Pehrsson, Allen, Folger, McMillen, & Lowe, 2007) who have mastered neither sophisticated rational thinking nor the linguistic competencies that will emerge in their later teen years (Pardeck, 1994; Vuchinich, Angelelli, & Gatherum, 1996). But preadolescents do have their own personal narratives. They have their own life stories, and they need to tell them in ways that are different from adults. Counselors can help youngsters access their own narratives and do so in some very creative ways through journaling, letter writing, poetry (Mazza, 2003), cinema therapy, therapeutic storytelling, drama therapy (R. A. Gardner, 1992; Gladding, 2011), and bibliotherapy interventions (Heath, Sheen, Leavy, Young, & Money, 2005; Shrodes, 1950). Counselors can assist children by introducing them to the narratives of others and also by guiding them in the telling of their own stories. Narratives, especially biographical works, can enhance youngsters' understanding of and even identification with others who have had experiences similar to their own; as a result of this, a sense of normalcy can develop (Jasmine-DeVias, 1995; Pardeck & Pardeck, 1993, 1998). Advantages to using narratives also include a diminished sense of isolation, an enhanced sense of cultural or ethnic pride, and generation of and exposure to alternative solutions and problem-solving strategies (Hynes & Hynes-Berry, 1994; Pardeck, 2005). Children are "wired" socially to learn from stories, which makes narrative approaches useful tools for counselors (Crenshaw, 2004).

Narratives can be established through either receptive or expressive activities. Receptive narrative activities might include reading, listening, and watching. These receptive activities result in helping children to establish an internal sense of their personal narratives. Expressive narratives activities could involve writing; telling; creating; and, of course, movement such as signing, gesturing, and engaging in other communicative acts. Indeed, when receptive and expressive activities are combined, original narratives will emerge (Crenshaw, 2004; R. A. Gardner, 1992). Such narrative creations can be developed into highly effective counseling techniques. As clients develop a narrative plot with characters, settings, and most of all actions, they can try out new strategies; discover feelings that may not have been accessible otherwise; and enjoy a sense of creation, control, and empowerment.

In this chapter, we use two techniques to illustrate how narrative can be used for assessment and group work to help youngsters move toward a healthy sense of autonomy. These are the Co-story-ing technique (Pehrsson, 2007) and the Language Fantasy Approach (LFA; Pehrsson & Pehrsson, 2007). Furthermore, the counselor in this case study uses a case journaling technique to inform her practice and counseling work.

The Case of Tiffany

First Meeting

A sixth-grade student knocked gently on the partially open door. Ms. Charlotte Stephanos, the school counselor, opened the door and welcomed Tiffany, who stepped inside cautiously while looking straight ahead. Tiffany stood still in the center of the room and folded her arms tight about her gray wool coat. Charlotte introduced herself to Tiffany and invited her to sit in the chair next to the desk. With arms still folded, Tiffany sat straight up in the chair. Charlotte asked Tiffany if she wished to remove her coat, but Tiffany shook her head and said, "I want to keep my coat on. I'm cold."

Charlotte responded, "Okay. Sounds like a plan. You decided to keep on your coat."

Then Tiffany asked, "Why am I here? My English teacher just told me to come to this office right now. She wouldn't tell me why or anything."

"Well, Ms. Baker and some of your other teachers are concerned about you and thought maybe I could help. They think you may need to talk with someone. They really want to help you. They think maybe you have some worries."

Tiffany shook her head and said, "I don't want help, and I don't want to talk about anything. I do not have *worries*." Tiffany emphasized the word *worries* by slowly lengthening it as if making fun of it. Then she sighed deeply as if the word annoyed her. "There's nothing wrong with me. I'm perfect!" She tightened her arms about her coat and asked, "Can I go now?"

"Yes, you can," responded Charlotte. "But I would like to meet with you again in two days. Let's see what time works."

"Whatever!" Tiffany said, as she rose from her chair.

Opening her appointment book, Charlotte said, "Thursday at this time seems to work. Ms. Baker won't mind if you come and see me during her English class."

Tiffany said, "Whatever." She nodded her head in agreement and exited the office.

Charlotte watched as Tiffany walked slowly down the hall with her arms tight around her waist. Tiffany's coat seemed molded to her like a suit of armor.

Background Information

Tiffany had been referred to Charlotte Stephanos, the school counselor, by the sixth-grade teaching team. However, according to an anecdotal paper written by her fifth-grade teacher, Tiffany's behavior had changed slowly. At first her work had been excellent and she had been popular among the other students. But then she withdrew socially and her work performance began to suffer. By the end of the school year Tiffany was avoiding contact with the other youngsters. During that time Tiffany usually chose to sit alone on a bench in the back of the lunchroom. During the past month or two she had no longer been completing her homework, and her grades were in a sharp decline.

At the end of the school year she was tested by Dr. Friedman, the school psychologist. According to his report Tiffany's scores indicated that her IQ was within the high normal range. However, the report also indicated that Tiffany was often reluctant to respond and appeared to be afraid to make mistakes. Although she appeared to have strong potential, as indicated by Dr. Friedman's report and other reports in her cumulative folder, Tiffany was presently failing all major subjects.

Prior to meeting with Tiffany, Charlotte thought it would be wise to consult with one of her teachers. That afternoon she met with Tiffany's English teacher. Ms. Baker agreed to allow Tiffany to go to the counseling office on Thursday. She said, "I think she needs you more than she needs homonyms." Then Ms. Baker added, "I met with Tiffany's mother about two weeks ago. She was concerned about Tiffany's schoolwork. Her mother reported, 'Tiffany takes a long time to do her homework,' but I told her that Tiffany seldom hands in any homework at all. Her mother also said, 'Tiffany is very well behaved at home but recently she seems to be a bit withdrawn. She spends much of her time in her room with her door locked.'"

Charlotte asked, "What about her social life? Does she have friends?"

Ms. Baker replied, "No, I don't think so. I never see her with anyone else, and her mother seemed to indicate that Tiffany likes to be alone. She has two younger brothers and she babysits them. Her only friend is Peter."

"Peter?" asked Charlotte. "Is he in this school?"

"No. Peter is the family dog. Apparently her mother and father go out a lot. Her mother hinted that Tiffany's father has a little bit of a drinking problem. Tiffany's mother said she accompanies him so he doesn't drink as much. She also said she drinks a little just to keep him in check. She thinks that helps him. She also stated that they have recently become very involved with their church, and that seems to be helping."

Charlotte walked slowly back to her office. Tiffany puzzled her, and under such circumstances she usually found it helpful to dialogue with herself in writing. When she returned to the counseling office, Charlotte pulled out her journal and began to write.

> ### Counselor Journal Entry 1
>
> *Tiffany's behavior changed last year when she was in fifth grade. Why? Well, I don't know yet, but I'll assume that her behavior is a way of responding to some other concern that may be related to changing relationships perhaps in part because of her developmental stage. Did something change in her home or in school? Her relationships changed at about the same time that her schoolwork declined. Is she having relationship problems with others, such as her friends, her parents, her other family members? Well, maybe she isn't having problems with others as much as she's having a relationship problem with herself.*
>
> *Maybe that's her problem. Maybe she doesn't feel that she fits in her world.*
>
> *At least part of her problem seems to involve relationships. I need to investigate more about this. Well, first I need to get her view of the story. What events or what else changed in her story? Yes! That's what I'll do on Thursday. I'll uncover her story.*

Second Meeting

Tiffany entered the counseling office, closed the door, and then locked it. Charlotte looked up from her desk, smiled, and beckoned Tiffany to come further into the room. Tiffany, with her gray coat wrapped tightly around her body, walked past the table in the center of the room and sat in the chair on the side of Charlotte's desk. Charlotte asked, "Would you like to sit at the table so we can talk, or would you prefer to stay here?"

Tiffany shrugged, "It's okay here."

Charlotte asked, "Could you tell me about yourself? I mean what are some of the things you like to do?"

Tiffany grimaced and shrugged. "Not much. I like to read novels, but that's all. I don't like to do much."

"You like to read novels. Tell me about the novels you read."

"Not much to tell. I just read about . . . I don't know. Nothing . . . really."

"Can you tell me what kind of stories you like to read?"

"No. I don't want to talk about that. I don't want to talk about anything. Can I leave now?"

Charlotte smiled and said, "Of course you can leave, but maybe you would like to talk about something else. For example, can you tell me about your family or your friends?"

"I really don't want to talk about my family, and I don't have any friends. I'm really missing a lot in English class, so can I leave now?"

"Certainly, but I would like to see you again on Monday. Would you like to come at a different time? I can arrange for you to come during your social studies class."

Tiffany shrugged, rose from the chair, said, "Whatever." She walked out of the office and down the school hall.

Counselor Journal Entry 2

Well, as the poet Burns said, "The best laid plans of mice and . . ."—hmm, and women, too. I did not even get close to Tiffany's story. She's like a turtle locking her head and limbs deep in her shell. For both turtles and people, fear is usually their reason for withdrawing into their safe shells.

I did find out something about Tiffany. Even though she shows an attitude, she knows how to be polite: She knocked on the open door. She likes to read novels. Reading fiction can be a sign of withdrawal from her real world. And then there's her English class. I wonder if she really likes that class or she just wanted to use it as an excuse for getting out of here. Homonyms? Why would a 12-year-old like homonyms? Poetry? I wonder if she would like to write her story. Perhaps by entering into a fantasy with her I can help her explore more freely and then help her find a way back to dealing with her situational issues.

Charlotte remembered a technique from graduate school called Co-story-ing (Pehrsson, 2007). This technique is particularly appropriate for use with preadolescents who are reclusive, nonverbal, and withdrawn. The counselor and client coconstruct a narrative and through this process create a client-centered story. This counseling intervention gives the child an opportunity to explore feelings and to test out consequences of behaviors in a narrative world, one far less threatening than the child's real world. Co-story-ing allows the counselor to slowly build trust and eventually uncover the child's early maladaptive schemas that frame the core issue.

Third Meeting

Charlotte got right to the point: "You told me you like to read novels. Why don't we write a story?"

Tiffany shook her head and said, "I don't spell very well, so I only write stories for myself."

"Well, correct spelling is not all that important. It's the ideas and an exciting plot that matters, and most of all interesting characters." Charlotte swiveled her chair over to a table with a computer on it. Tiffany turned her chair to see the monitor. There were two keyboards attached, and Charlotte placed one in front of Tiffany.

Tiffany said, "I don't know how to start a story."

"No problem! I'll start," said Charlotte as she wrote: *One time, a very long time ago in a far distant place there was . . .* Charlotte looked at Tiffany and said, "Your turn."

Tiffany placed her fingers on the keyboard and typed: *an exploshun.*

Charlotte typed: *And everybody . . .*

Tiffany: *ran. They were scared.*

Charlotte: *They didn't know what . . .*

Tiffany: *happened. Three of them hid in . . .*

Charlotte: *a cave. One of them had an idea.*

Tiffany: *That was Nancy and she decided to go back to the house that exploded.*

Charlotte: *She wanted to see . . .*

Tiffany: *if her parents were still alive.*

Charlotte: *She hoped . . .*

Tiffany: *they were dead.* Then Tiffany quickly backspaced over the last word and typed: *alive.*

Charlotte: *Nancy went to the house and . . .*

Tiffany: *her father was really, really mad at her for blowing up the house.*

Charlotte: *Her father . . .*

Tiffany: *blamed it all on Nancy because she always doing bad things.*

Charlotte: *Then the other two . . .*

Tiffany: *came out of the cave and they came to the exploded house.*

Charlotte: *Then her father . . .*

Tiffany: *got even more angry because she left her two brothers alone in the cave.*

Charlotte: *Then Nancy . . .*

Tiffany: *promised to be good always and never to use bad words and to blow up the house again.*

Tiffany looked up from the monitor, shrugged, grimaced as if with pain, and typed: *The End!*

Charlotte said, "We wrote a story!"

Tiffany said, "Can I go back to class now?"

As Tiffany walked out of the office, Charlotte was already writing in her dialogue journal.

Counselor Journal Entry 3

I think Tiffany gave me her story! At least I have some clues that I need to follow up on. I think Nancy represents Tiffany, and if that is so, then Tiffany thinks of herself as being bad. But more than that, she is struggling against her father's or parents' authority. I'm not surprised that her story involved hiding in a cave. The story ends with some ambiguity: Does she or does she not want to blow up the house again? It is time for me to talk with Tiffany's parents. I'll try calling. At any rate, after three sessions, I need to get parental permission as well.

Later that day Charlotte telephoned Mrs. Knapp, Tiffany's mother, and told her that Tiffany had attended three sessions with her and that she would like to continue working with Tiffany. Mrs. Knapp asked why Tiffany was seeing a counselor. Charlotte explained that Tiffany had been referred by her teachers and that they had felt she could use some help. Her schoolwork seemed to be suffering, and they wanted to know why. Tiffany had stopped handing in her homework a couple of months ago. Maybe she was worried about something that was interfering with her grades.

Mrs. Knapp said, "We have noticed that Tiffany has changed. She had been an absolutely perfect and responsible child until several months ago. We are hoping it's just a stage, perhaps the onset of puberty, and she'll get over it. Tiffany does spend a lot of time alone, and we thought she had a lot of homework. But last week my husband walked into her bedroom and found her reading a novel. He was very annoyed and took the book away from her. He thinks novels are a waste of time. He now keeps careful watch over her to make sure she is doing her homework and not wasting time." Mrs. Knapp further explained, "My husband and I became very concerned about her last year because her friends were—well, how can

I say this?—just not good influences on her. We overheard them talking, and she was using words that we had never expected her to use."

When Charlotte prompted her for examples of these words, Mrs. Knapp said, "Well, you know, vulgar words, even words that take the name of the Lord in vain. My husband read her text messages, and we know what OMG stands for. We took her cell phone away from her. Then we overheard Tiffany and her friends using impolite language. She and her friends were constantly telling one another to shut up. We don't allow such rude behavior in our family."

Mrs. Knapp mentioned again that Tiffany had been an ideal child but that within the past year she had become irresponsible and rebellious. "My husband likes a few drinks once in a while, but, don't get me wrong, he's not an alcoholic—at least not anymore. We have a favorite church club, and it's Tiffany's responsibility to babysit her younger brothers because it's important that I have a drink or two with my husband. But the boys run wild when we're out, and once Timmy got hurt and was bleeding when we got home, and it was Tiffany's fault. She was spending her time reading novels and talking with her friends on the phone instead of watching the boys. We have had to put a stop to that."

After the phone conversation, Charlotte quickly opened her dialogue journal and began to write.

Counselor Journal Entry 4

First I should consider relationships. Tiffany's relationship with her parents seems to have changed recently; should I say drastically? Her parents are making more demands on her and placing limitations on her at the very time that she is trying to develop her identity and autonomy as an individual. Tiffany has a basic need to make decisions for herself, particularly at her developmental stage.

What about other relationships? I can understand why Tiffany has no friends. Not only have her parents set limits that seem unreasonable, but they do not seem to understand that Tiffany needs to use the language of her own culture. That culture is a developmental one, that of her young preadolescent peers or her 'tween friends. This leads me to hypothesize that Tiffany could be responding to a core issue of unrelenting standards, but so far I am not able to discern whether her style is one of avoidance or surrender.

I'll call back and explain these things to Tiffany's mother, and that should help.

The next day Charlotte again called Tiffany's mother and explained to her that Tiffany's developmental needs seemed to be conflicting with some of her parents' demands. Mrs. Knapp agreed that Tiffany was in a certain developmental stage—she called it "a rebellious stage." She explained that her husband had recently been ordained a deacon in their church and that he knew very well how their daughter should be treated during this rebellious stage. In fact, he counseled parents about how they should deal with their rebellious children. Mrs. Knapp agreed that Tiffany should continue to meet with Charlotte, but she told Charlotte that she and her husband expected her to help Tiffany overcome her rebellious attitude and work through this stage.

Counselor Journal Entry 5

So this is in some way a developmental issue, but Tiffany's development is being blocked by the unrelenting standards that are being imposed by the home environment. This is clearly a "problem with others" situation, and the implications for Tiffany could be profound. It's clear that Tiffany is not able to change her environment and is unable to change the situational condition, so she is choosing an emotional path of surrendering to the obstacles imposed by her parents and avoiding by withdrawing from others and from school-related activity. Before I can be certain about my hypothesis, however, I'll try another Co-story-ing assessment with Tiffany and see what unfolds.

Fourth Meeting

The next day, Tiffany, wearing her coat but this time unbuttoned, again knocked on Charlotte's door. She immediately agreed to write another story with Charlotte. Charlotte started with: *It was a dark and dreary night and . . .* The story unfolded from there. Tiffany took control. Her story was about a teenage girl, Lori, who had been camping with her parents but went for a hike by herself and got lost in the forest. Unable to find her way back to the camp, Lori wandered for hours until dark. She was chilled to the bone. Deep in the forest she saw a warm fire and discovered another campsite. These campers were all teenagers. They were from a far-off magic land and spoke another language. Lori made friends and learned their language. She changed her name to Stephanie and stayed there.

Counselor Journal Entry 6

Tiffany's story adds evidence to my hypothesis that she is engaged in a developmentally appropriate endeavor of striving for autonomy and even for her very identity, but her parents are blocking her development, resulting in a core issue related to unrelenting standards. Her teachers see Tiffany as a loner, but that may be because she is using either a surrender or a avoidance coping strategy in response to her parents. Tiffany appears to be longing for friendships, so at this point I am leaning more toward an avoidance response style than one of surrender. Tiffany does seem to enjoy writing and is becoming more comfortable with this process. During this session Tiffany had her coat on, but it was unbuttoned and she did not fold her arms around her. This is a positive sign. Perhaps she is feeling less of a need to protect herself here. I've been working with three other girls in a group, and one just moved away. I'll give Tiffany the choice of joining the group or continuing to meet with me alone. I prefer to work with a group of three because the group dynamics work best in such situations (Pardeck & Pardeck, 1984).

Later that day, Charlotte saw Tiffany in the hall and asked, "Tiffany, would you like to meet in my office tomorrow with two other girls?"

Tiffany shuddered and asked, "Who are they?"

Charlotte answered, "I think you know them—Jasmine and Henrietta. They are in a different sixth-grade class, so I thought . . ."

Tiffany wrapped her coat tight around her but said, "I know them. Okay. Whatever."

Charlotte had carefully chosen the other two youngsters to work in a group with Tiffany because they seemed to have some common core issues.

Counselor Journal Entry 7

These three children—Tiffany, Jasmine, and Henrietta—are experiencing challenges in developing autonomy. Their parents all seem to be—how should I say it?—placing major limitations on their behavior. These preadolescents have something else in common: They enjoy reading fiction. This suggests the use of an intervention related to bibliotherapy (Pardeck, 1994, 1998).

Books are used in a bibliotherapy approach, but most of the research has focused on books that are expository and informational in nature (Pehrsson & McMillen, 2005). Counselors surveyed in 2008 indicated that they use mostly informational and self-help materials with clients (Pehrsson & McMillen, 2009). Although children do need content, Tiffany, Jasmine, and Henrietta were likely to benefit far more from narratives. They would benefit from sharing their narratives and learning from the narratives of others (both shared within the group or drawn from the pages of a story). They had a need to develop strategies to cope with their environments at a time when they really could not change their situations. Moreover, they needed to develop identities that allowed for autonomy. They also needed an avenue for socializing, because identity emerges within a social environment. Therefore, it would have been best if they could be more active within a group experience in which each child could be free to develop an identity that was more capable of coping within restricted environments. One intervention that works well with groups and preadolescents is the LFA (Pehrsson & Pehrsson, 2007).

Among other beneficial outcomes, the LFA helps develop autonomy. In the LFA, "each child is responsible for the actions of one character who works cooperatively with the other characters as they journey to solve problems, to meet challenges, to deal with threats and to return triumphant to their home" (Pehrsson & Pehrsson, 2007, p. 42). This is a typical theme within some culturally based myths (see Campbell, 1968). The LFA also helps a child develop alternative means of engaging, establishing a positive role identity, becoming responsible, and taking on appropriate risks. As the characters develop strategies and constitute strong identities, so do the children. Risks in this procedure have consequences, and inappropriate risks usually have negative consequences as the fantasy unfolds. Pehrsson and Pehrsson (2007) stressed the value of this approach when they wrote:

> Fantasy is a typical component of a group counseling session during which children involve themselves in an adventurous story where each character meets, struggles, deals with, and overcomes challenges. As their characters learn to work cooperatively, so do the children. (p. 42)

Myth, especially for children, is not far from the real, or as Levi-Strauss (1979) stated, "For me it [the myth] describes a lived experience" (p. 3). According to Rollo May (1991), "Myths are archetypical patterns in human consciousness. . . . Where there is consciousness, there will be myth" (p. 3). The LFA involves a child in more than just reading myths about heroes; "each child lives an experience with a character as an alter ego that eventually is assimilated into the original ego" (Pehrsson & Pehrsson, 2007, p. 42).

First Group Session

Tiffany, Jasmine, and Henrietta entered the counseling office at about the same time and each sat with arms folded. Tiffany's coat was wrapped tightly within her folded arms.

Charlotte got right to the point. "What kinds of stories do you like? Jasmine you tell us first."

Jasmine responded, "I don't know. Uh . . . maybe, uh . . ." She looked around at the many books on the shelves and said, "I like a good mystery."

Henrietta chimed in, "I hate boring stories. I like adventure stories."

The two girls looked at Tiffany, who said, "Whatever."

Charlotte smiled and said, "Okay! Let's get started. It sounds like we agree on an adventurous mystery." Charlotte then set a keyboard and a small computer screen in front of each youngster. With excitement in her voice, she said, "How should we begin an exciting mystery story?"

Henrietta said, "Let's write about a camping trip, and there's a storm and some really bad people—"

Jasmine interrupted, "That's good and the bad people are vampires."

Henrietta added, "And they can be a family of vampires, and they only come out of their tent at night."

Charlotte said, "Great ideas! I like that. It sounds pretty scary. What do you think, Tiffany?"

After a moment of silence, Tiffany stated, "Whatever."

Charlotte prompted Tiffany, "Should we start the story at night or during the day?"

Tiffany said, "Whatever."

Charlotte said to Tiffany, "You get to choose if the story starts during the day or at night."

Tiffany responded, "During the day or . . . whatever." Then she added, "Twilight."

Charlotte said, "Good! We'll start the story during twilight at the campsite."

Jasmine said, "It's just getting dark and the family is fixing a fire."

Charlotte responded, "Yes! And how about if there are three teenage girls, and they just met each other that day when their families arrived at the camp?"

The three girls nodded in agreement, and Tiffany added, "They got to be friends right away. And they're all from New York City, but the camp is upstate in, like, the mountains."

Charlotte encouraged, "What a great idea! Yes! Let's give them names. What names should we give our story characters? You each get to choose one name."

Jasmine chose the name Marissa. Henrietta wanted her character to be called Sofia. But Tiffany wanted to call her character Tiffany. Charlotte gently urged her to consider a name that differed from her own, and after several suggestions, including a computer search of girls' names, followed by several "whatevers," Tiffany chose Isabel as the name of her character.

"Now we can begin. Let's decide together the best way to start our story," said Charlotte.

Jasmine said, "What about you? You should have a name and be in the story. Maybe you could be one of the vampires."

Charlotte said, "Well, if we need another character I could join in, but we each get to decide who we are, and I certainly don't want to be a vampire."

Jasmine added, "Shouldn't we decide how the story will end before we begin?"

Charlotte said, "I think it's more fun if we just start our mystery adventure and see where it takes us."

After some further discussion about how the story would unfold, Tiffany, in a very low voice, suggested, "It was a dark and dreary twilight."

"And three teenagers sat around the campfire," Henrietta added. "I know how to make a campfire because I'm a Girl Scout."

Jasmine said, "Me too! We belong to the same troop."

Without saying anything, Tiffany typed the first half of the sentence: *It was a dark and dreery twylite*

Henrietta added: *and three teanagers sat around the camp fire.* Then Henrietta said, "I think I spelled some of the words wrong."

Charlotte said, "That's okay. We can edit spelling and other stuff after we get our ideas down first." Then Charlotte suggested, "Maybe there's a problem. Like maybe something really special and magical was stolen from the campsite, and the girls are talking about how they can be detectives and get it back."

"It could be a ring, and it's a magic ring," suggested Henrietta. "Or maybe it's a statue of a soldier who guards and protects the campsite."

The girls agreed that the statue that protected the campsite had been stolen and that they would have to try to find it.

Then Charlotte looked at Jasmine and said, "So, Marissa, what are you doing?"

Jasmine said, "Hmmm. Let me see. I'm looking at the tent with the vampires because maybe they stole the statue."

Henrietta said, "But we don't know they're vampires yet."

Jasmine said, "Somebody ran through the campsite and stole the statue, and suddenly there was a great big storm."

Henrietta added, "And the cars won't start and the cell phones and iPods and nothing works because the statue was stolen."

Charlotte said, "Good! How are you going to write that in our story?"

Jasmine added the second sentence: *Suddenly a huge bat flew down and picked up a statue at the entrance to the campsite.*

Henrietta typed: *Then a terrific wind came and thunder and lightning crashed all around.*

Jasmine added: *All the cell phones went dead and it got really cold and some men tried to start their cars but all the batteries were dead. Marissa saw a light go on in the tent near a cave. Marissa said, "Look at that tent. The light is on. This looks mysteryus."*

Henrietta typed: *Then a boy comes out of the tent and Sofia thought he was really cute.*

After Henrietta typed this, Charlotte looked at Tiffany and said, "What is Isabel doing?"

Tiffany folded her arms tight around her coat and said, "I don't know."

Charlotte asked, "Does she say something about the new guy? Does she look at him and smile, or does she get up and fix the fire?"

Tiffany said, "She fixes the fire . . . or . . . whatever."

Charlotte responds, "Okay! Write what Isabel does."

Tiffany typed: *Isabel got up and fixed the fire.*

Henrietta immediately added to the story by typing: *The cute guy came over to the three teanagers and said, Good evening, my name is Ivan. I am from Transilvanya. What are your names?*

Henrietta looked up and said, "I think I need some quotation marks, but I don't know where."

Charlotte repeated her previous advice. "Let's not worry about editing and stuff like that. We can edit later." Then she turned to Tiffany and asked, "What will Isabel do? Will she tell Ivan her name?"

Tiffany wrote: *I'm Isabel.*

Charlotte asked, "We have to decide what Ivan will do next. Do you think he should do something scary, or should he be nice and polite or what?"

Tiffany said, "He'll be nice and polite because he wants to trap the girls and suck their blood, so he's nice and polite so they trust him and then he'll make them into vampires."

"Great idea!" said Charlotte, as Jasmine and Henrietta smiled and nodded in agreement.

As their story progressed, Ivan asked Marissa, Sofia, and Isabel to come to his tent because he knew where the statue was, but when they entered, two other vampires grabbed them and took them through the back of the tent into the deep winding tunnels of the cave. The vampires locked them in a cage.

When the session was over, Charlotte suggested that they end their first exciting episode with: *To be continued.* After they quickly edited the spelling and some "other stuff," Charlotte printed four copies. They agreed to write the next exciting episode on Thursday. As the three girls walked together back to their classrooms they were talking about what would happen in their next episode. Charlotte heard Tiffany say, "Whatever." But then again, Tiffany actually seemed to be contributing to the therapeutic conversation.

Counselor Journal Entry 8

The task in which I am engaged is supporting the development of autonomy and identity. This is a disquieting issue for all three girls but of major concern for Tiffany. The LFA provides opportunities to address both issues. Two of the girls, Henrietta and Jasmine, demonstrated some beginnings of autonomy as I provided acceptance and more than that, as Carl Rogers would call it, unconditional positive regard. Autonomy develops from freedom to function and making decisions without being criticized. Today I avoided any kind of criticism, including correcting spelling and grammar during the creative part of the process. Editing and creating do not fit well together; editing can kill creativity. Therefore, they are best dealt with as separate tasks, and one should follow the other.

Identity develops in situations and includes risk. Tiffany is not open to taking risks. I have assessed this to be a function of her response to the unrelenting standards core issue imposed within her home environment. Her contributions to the story were very safe. Her constant use of the term "whatever" could mean that she does not care or, more likely, it could be part of her strategy to give away her power by choice so as to avoid being caught failing to live up to yet another standard in her young life.

This process of engaging in story creation could help Tiffany differentiate between the nature of the home environment and that of the outside world and thereby support an identity that allows her to cope with her present situation as well as the challenges that inevitably will come her way. She appears to be afraid to take risks. Her parents have limited her social life, but she needs friendships to develop her own identity.

Tiffany expressed, through Isabel, a desire to socialize with other girls, but she needs to do so in a way that is acceptable to her parents. She seems to be letting down some of her defenses with Jasmine and Henrietta. Perhaps friendships will emerge.

Second Group Session

The three girls returned, and each held their copy of the first chapter. Their first order of business was to give their story a title.

Jasmine suggested *The Vampire Cave.*

They agreed to that title, and then Charlotte suggested that the girls read their own parts of the first episode like a play. Jasmine and Henrietta immediately agreed.

Tiffany protested, "I don't like to read aloud."

Charlotte asked Tiffany, "Would you feel better if you prepared reading your parts first to yourself? It's what actors do. They don't just read their parts without preparation. Actually, I don't think we should ever read aloud without preparation. It can be scary."

Tiffany said, "Tell that to our teachers."

Then each of the girls, guided by Charlotte, underlined the part she would practice and then read as part of a play. Charlotte suggested that they tape-record their play and even make sound effects like a radio program or a story track on an MP3 player. The girls then practiced reading their parts and decided how to make sound effects. For example, by tapping a pencil on the recorder they made a sound like someone was walking, and when they tapped faster it resembled someone running. They wrinkled paper to make the sound of walking through leaves. The wrinkling of paper also sounded like the campfire.

After they read and recorded their first episode, Charlotte asked, "What will Marissa, Sofia, and Isabel do now that they are locked in that cage deep in that cave?"

Tiffany said, "They should hide under blankets or maybe just call for help."

Jasmine said, "I think Ivan could help them because maybe he's a good vampire and he doesn't drink people's blood. He has a special medicine he drinks."

Henrietta suggested, "Sofia has a big hairpin and she knows how to pick a lock, so she could get them out."

After some discussion it was decided. Sofia picked the lock and the girls got out of the cage. They tried to find their way out of the cave, but they kept getting lost in the winding tunnels. They found a skeleton.

Tiffany wrote: *Isabel shouted and called for help.*

Jasmine immediately typed: *Marissa heard the vampires running toward them. Be quiet. They know we got out of the cage.*

Henrietta wrote: *Suddenly a huge bat flew into the tunnel and landed in front of them. It turned into one of the vampires.*

Charlotte said, "That's great and very exciting! Time is up, but we can write more next Tuesday." She typed: *To be continued.*

Charlotte watched as the girls walked down the school hall. She could hear them discussing ideas for the next episode. Then she just barely heard Tiffany say something about Ivan. She didn't know what she said, but Henrietta and Jasmine nodded their heads and seemed to like the idea.

Counselor Journal Entry 9

I am constantly tempted to suggest ideas for the story, but I must realize the purpose of this approach does not include writing a great work of fiction, or even a good one. This is their story, not mine. The story will proceed with my very limited participation. I do have difficulty with this because, as a former English teacher, I really would like to instruct these girls in story writing, but I will resist that temptation. Of course, I will absolutely resist any correcting while they are constructing their story, and I will offer help only with minor edits.

Based on their experiences and research, Pehrsson and Pehrsson (2007) observed a pattern of three stages to the LFA. The first involves the counselor helping youngsters establish and situate the story characters. The counselor accepts and even affirms the right of each youngster to control his or her own character in the story. This sounds very permissive, and it is. However, as I can see from Tiffany's shout for help, consequences emerge from within the story and are supported by the group process. This is far better than a counselor's cautions, or perhaps over-protectiveness. I should always trust that the consequences of poor decisions will emerge from the story itself and its subsequent enactment and not from any hint of my cautioning or criticizing.

At this stage each youngster and her story character are separate, and the make-believe world is distant and therefore safe. The characters usually can risk dangers.

However, when a youngster needs to make a decision about a character, there may be risk and a typical response is "I don't know." When in the first session Tiffany responded this way, to get her involved I provided her with choices of how she could respond, and she did choose one. Pehrsson and Pehrsson (2007) suggest that when a youngster says "I don't know," the counselor offer three suggestions, two involving accepting a challenge and one of avoidance. Tiffany chose avoidance by having Isabel fix the fire. This provides additional support for an avoidance coping response to her core issue.

Perhaps Tiffany will begin to trust more as this story progresses. I still think she needs to socialize with youngsters her age, and maybe Jasmine and Henrietta can provide some help in that regard.

Third Group Session

Again the girls practiced reading their parts and then audiotaped their story with sound effects. Tiffany seemed much more relaxed with this process. Jasmine told Charlotte that they were becoming friends and that they sat together at lunch. Tiffany smiled, nodded her head, and said, "Jasmine and Henrietta go to the same church as me . . . as I do. So we're going to meet Sunday morning and attend services together." Then the girls took their places around the table in front of their computer monitors and keyboards. Tiffany had her coat on, but it was hanging loose and unbuttoned.

Charlotte asked, "What do you think will happen now that the vampire has flown into the tunnel?"

Jasmine immediately answered, "I think it's Ivan and he's come to help them escape from the bloodsucking vampires."

Henrietta and Tiffany agreed, and Jasmine began typing her sentence.

Initially the episode developed with Marissa, Sofia, and Isabel depending on Ivan to rescue them. He led them to another opening in the cave. But when they came out they were in a totally different forest. It was more like a jungle with strange animals and bright red trees, a sort of parallel universe.

Tiffany wrote: *Isabel looked all around and said, "I don't think we're in New York anymore."*

Henrietta wrote: *Sofia said, "I don't think we're on earth anymore."*

Charlotte suggested that Ivan should return to the cave because it was morning and the sun was coming up. But Marissa, Sofia, and Isabel had a problem: They could not find their way back to the campsite. They got lost again in the deep, dark, mysterious jungle with very strange trees and animals. It looked like a totally different world.

Jasmine wrote: *Suddenly Marissa heard a loud chattering right under her feet. She looked down and saw big rotten scary teeth.*

Charlotte said, "That's really scary. Isabel, what are you going to do?"

Tiffany wrote: *A skeleton with big ugly rotten teeth was going to bite Marissa but Isabel jumped on its head and screamed. The skeleton sank back down under the ground.*

Charlotte said, "Wow! Isabel jumped on its head! That was brave."

Jasmine smiled at Tiffany, nodded her head, and wrote: *Thanks, Isabel, you saved my life.*

Henrietta wrote: *Then Sofia saw another skeleton coming out of the ground. She shouted, "They are skeleton zombies!"*

Then Charlotte suggested that they continue their story next Thursday. Once again Charlotte printed three copies of the episode and gave one to each girl. As the girls started walking down the hall, Charlotte turned and saw a gray coat on one of the chairs. She picked it up and called to Tiffany. Tiffany returned for her coat, which she placed over her arm. She then ran back to catch up with Jasmine and Henrietta.

Counselor Journal Entry 10

Tiffany seems to have made friends, and they may be acceptable to her parents. Also, Tiffany seems to have entered into the second stage of the LFA. Her character, Isabel, is becoming brave. She is taking appropriate risks, developing autonomy, and beginning to develop a positive identity. Such changes are encouraging in that they are more characteristic of a compensation coping strategy, which will better support Tiffany's growth and development in venues outside the home.

While we were writing the story, Tiffany's coat came off, and I didn't even notice until she had left it behind. I think not only is Isabel becoming braver but Tiffany is letting down her protective armor, symbolized by her coat. The next stage would be for Tiffany to identify more directly with her character in the story and take on some of her resilient characteristics. If this is happening after only three sessions, it means that Tiffany is making progress very rapidly. My message to the youngster at the second stage is that your character is becoming braver, but the message for the third stage is that you are becoming braver. Tiffany's character, Isabel, is becoming brave, but it will likely take some more time for Tiffany to make similar progress. Then again, her coat came off, so it will be interesting to see the pace at which she unfolds. In our next sessions I will focus on Tiffany as the decision maker. I'll start talking to the characters and use their names as I address the girls. That should help them identify with their characters and take a step toward authorship of their own living story. I will make some suggestions to include challenges for their characters and to encourage appropriate risks. However, if they choose inappropriate risks, the consequences should play out naturally in the story.

Fourth Group Session

After the girls practiced reading their parts of the third episode and audio-recorded the radio play, they sat in front of their keyboards ready to write their fourth episode of *The Vampire Cave.*

Jasmine said, "I've been thinking about these skeleton zombies. They give me the shivers. They are really scary!"

Henrietta put up her hand and waved it in front of Jasmine. She said, "It's only a make-believe story."

Charlotte suggested, "Let's begin and see what Marissa, Sofia, and Isabel do about them. What are you going to do, Isabel?"

The three girls smiled when Charlotte called Tiffany Isabel. Then each girl assumed the names of their characters as they contributed by typing the following sentences.

Tiffany wrote: *When Isabel jumped on the skeleton zombie's head, it came off and rolled down a hill. Isabel laughed and said, "OMG!"*

Sofia said, *"LOL! That's how we can get rid of these zombies. Kick them in their skulls."*

Tiffany typed: *Isabel saw three skeleton zombies coming out of the ground and she ran over and kicked each one and their skulls came off and went rolling down the hill onto a road.*

Marissa chuckled and said, *"The zombies can't see the girls because they have no heads. So they go around looking for their heads but we keep kicking their heads down the hill."*

As the episode continued along similar lines the girls giggled with joy. They increasingly included their text messaging language. Tiffany laughed loudly as they wrote about the girls kicking, heads rolling, and headless skeleton zombies wandering around the hilltop.

When the girls seemed to tire of this active scenario, *Sofia shouted, "Enough of this! Let's get out of here and find our campsite."*

Once again the three girls were off running down the hill, avoiding zombie heads and searching for their campsite.

Isabel said, *"It's getting dark again and the vampires will be out looking for us."*
Sofia said, *"Shut up!"*
Marissa said, *"It's twilight and there's a vampire right in front of us."*
Sofia turned around and there were *two vampires right in back of them.*

Charlotte said, "This is a very exciting episode, and you girls are really getting brave. I think it's time to write *'To be continued.'*"

Charlotte watched the three girls walk down the hall. It was then that she realized that Tiffany had not worn or even brought her coat to the counseling office.

Counselor Journal Entry 11

The story is taking on the characteristics of a typical myth. As described by Joseph Campbell (1968),

> *A hero ventures forth from the world of common day into a region of super-natural wonder: fabulous forces are there encountered and a decisive victory is won: the hero comes back from this mysterious adventure with the power to bestow boons on his fellow man. (p. 30)*

Campbell saw a hero as a male figure, but Kathleen Noble (1994) took exception to this conceptualization based on gender bias. Instead, Noble characterized the female hero as more likely to engage in cooperative work within the social group as opposed to a male archetype counterpart who might act alone and separate from a group.

The characters in the story are becoming very cooperative, and the girls sitting in my office are relaxing and enjoying themselves. Tiffany even laughed out loud. By bringing a sense of humor to their story the girls are releasing some anxiety, but, more than that, they are demonstrating a willingness to risk criticism from one another and also from me. Because Tiffany is holding a core issue of unrelenting standards, this is likely to be an increasingly important aspect to watch during these sessions. Her ability to respond to this type of interaction from peers without folding into an avoidant posture will be a key marker for the progress she makes during this narrative intervention. Of course, I do not intend to criticize any of their ideas or their language. Yet I understand that I would have to impose some limits under certain circumstances. For example, their characters cannot die. They cannot harm one another. Some other limitations, such as sex and violence, would involve my own judgment, but the girls are nowhere near approaching those limits.

I had concerns that the story characters would rely too much on others, such as Ivan, for help, but they are taking control and developing independence. This is a major step toward autonomy. It seems that Ivan, the vampire, has left the story. I see evidence that the girls themselves, not just their characters, are indeed developing coping strategies. I see the emergence of identities that will help them cope in a prosocial manner with their respective situational conditions. The text messaging words and expressions are an interesting inclusion. I wonder how Tiffany will handle the inclusion of their language because her parents are so opposed to what they consider to be inappropriate.

Fifth Group Session

Their fifth session began with the three girls running up a hill away from the three vampires. But the vampires turned into bats and flew to the top of the hill and waited for them. The girls rolled back down the hill, over the road, and onto another road, where they rolled into the front door of an abandoned country store. Isabel got up and ran to the grocery section, where she found three big rings of garlic. The girls put one around each of their necks and went to meet the vampires. The vampires ran away when they saw the garlic rings.

Marissa, Sofia, and Isabel continued to be lost in the forest. They met and overcame other challenges as they continued their search for the missing magic statue. By this time Charlotte was consistently using the names of the characters as they constructed their contributions to the story.

Sixth Group Session

Tiffany entered the counseling office before the other two girls arrived. She said, "Jasmine, Henrietta, and I went to church together on Sunday."

Charlotte asked, "Have you introduced the girls to your parents yet?"

Tiffany answered, "Not yet but they are coming to a backyard picnic at my house next Saturday. My mom and dad want to meet them."

Jasmine and Henrietta arrived, and the three girls started discussing their story. They agreed that Marissa, Sofia, and Isabel would have to find the missing statue and then find their way back to the campsite. They agreed that it was about time for the story to come to a conclusion.

Charlotte asked, "Sofia, what are you going to do?"

Without hesitation, Henrietta wrote: *Sofia said, "I think the statue is back in the cave. I remember I saw it in a corner when we were escaping and we have to go back there and find it but we have to go back through our escape opening in the cave."*

Marissa said, "The vampires probably have the magic statue and we can go in the cave and scare them off because we have the garlic."

Isabel said, "Let's go and get the magic statue."

The story continued with the girls entering the cave, scaring the vampires with their garlic, and finding the statue hidden in a corner. When they went back through the cave and out through the vampire tent, they arrived back at the campsite and to the world they recognized. The trees were green and the only animals they saw were chipmunks. The girls stopped writing at that point and discussed concerns about meeting their parents. Jasmine asked Charlotte, "How come it was okay for us to use the words and stuff we say in our text messaging? You never said we shouldn't say OMG and things like that."

Charlotte turned to her keyboard and wrote: *OIC. NP!* The girls giggled as Tiffany read from the monitor, "Oh I see. No problem!"

Jasmine immediately typed: *OMG! LOL!*

Henrietta said, "Shut up!"

Charlotte smiled and explained that the language people use among their own friends their own age (in the culture of preadolescent childhood) is not always the same as what they use when they are speaking to teachers, at church on Sunday, or with their parents. She further explained that some expressions that are acceptable within one group are not appropriate in another, so the girls would be wise to make sure they are not in a mixed group when they use the language that belongs in only one group. She said, "Your parents are not exactly in the same group to which you girls belong. Therefore, your parents may misinterpret what you say. For example, when you say 'Shut up,' your parents may think you are being rude, and when you write 'OMG,' they are likely to think that you are being disrespectful to God." Charlotte explained that friendship language is different from parent language and that word switching is appropriate.

Henrietta took the mouse, opened a blank document, and wrote: *My parents are GR8 about most things but I have to be careful about the way I talk. In front of my parents I have to be different. So if POS* [parent over shoulder]: *ssshhh.*

Charlotte said, "Yes! When we use our friendship language it's a good thing to think about using it just with our friends."

The girls agreed without any help from Charlotte to be careful about using their own language and to make informed decisions about the consequences when they use their friendship language in front of their parents. Jasmine looked at the clock on the wall and said, "We have only a couple of minutes. Let's finish our story."

After a short discussion, the girls agreed with Tiffany's suggestion "to finish the story with a weird and mysterious ending." Their story ended as follows:

When they went back through the cave and out through the vampire tent they arrived back at the campsite and to the world they recognized.

Marissa said, "We've been gone for days. I bet our parents are very worried."

The three girls ran up to their campsites. Their parents were still there but they were perfectly calm and they weren't worried.

Sofia asked, "Why weren't you worried about us? We were gone for days."

Their parents all looked like the girls were joking. They all looked at their watches and told the girls they had been gone for only about an hour.

The girls then held up the statue to show that they had found it and brought it back.

It was a very heavy statue so all three girls had to lift it back onto the pedestal. Suddenly the storm stopped and the stars came out and all the cell phones worked and the cars started. The next day they drove back to the city where they all lived.

The End

• • •

As the girls walked toward their classrooms, Charlotte could hear them talking. Jasmine and Henrietta were inviting Tiffany to join the Girl Scouts, and Tiffany was agreeing enthusiastically—no more "whatevers."

Counselor Journal Entry 12

Tiffany's character learned to cope with her situational conditions and changed her strategies for her emotion-focused coping. Her character, Isabel, developed autonomy and seemed to identify herself as brave and capable of taking appropriate risks. But more important, Tiffany has come out of her safe shell and has begun to abandon her avoidance coping style. She seems to be in the second stage of the LFA. As described by Pehrsson and Pehrsson (2007), this stage is achieved when "the child's character faces up to challenges and begins to develop creative ways to overcome monsters, villains or other problems" (p. 187). However, youngsters often regress back to the initial stage and avoid challenges; this is part of normal development.

I will continue to work with these three girls in a group, but I will arrange to see Tiffany individually for a few sessions. I will help her construct a bridge from the positive qualities of her story character to more successful coping strategies in her own life, which still has rigid and strictly imposed standards that are so inconsistent with the developmental stage of this young adolescent girl. I will help her to develop autonomy by encouraging her to take appropriate risks, to learn from less appropriate decisions, and to strengthen her decision-making process. I will show that I believe in her abilities to cope with her situational conditions while exhibiting the courage to act appropriately as she continues the process of differentiating between more and less restrictive relational environments.

Summary

This chapter has presented approaches to developing autonomy and identity through the use of story creating. The case of Tiffany is a composite of many similar experiences in the use of several forms of bibliotherapy with special focus on Co-story-ing and the LFA as a means of constituting a safe fictional world (Pehrsson, 2006; Pehrsson & Pehrsson, 2007).

We assume that a fictional world and the real world are not far removed, especially for children. Counselors can learn about a youngster's relational world, core issues, and coping strategies by creating, guiding, and cocreating a story that will most often parallel the client's actual world. Using an approach such as Co-story-ing is a way of gaining entrance into a client's psychological world; it provides a window to the client's schema. It provides for access to the child's world that is not psychologically blocked.

Rather than attempting to enter through a boarded up and heavily defended front entrance, one can use this approach to access content via the back door or, perhaps more likely, an unlocked basement window. Often the deepest and darkest concerns and fears can be uncovered when the counselor descends with the client into that basement filled with fears. Co-story-ing can provide access to scary places in the mind but with a safety net to make this exploration less threatening.

In addition, strategies developed and practiced in a fictional world can be transferred to the world of actual experiences. A fictive world can be a safe place for developing strategies, taking actions, and realizing consequences (Crenshaw, 2004; R. A. Gardner, 1992). Characters in a story will experience consequences, some of which may be unwanted, but in this setting the client is safe.

In the case presented here, as in many of our experiences writing stories with children, Tiffany, Jasmine, and Henrietta entered into a mythological world of their own. They created an archetypical story of heroes going forth into a foreign land to recover some object—in their case, a statue representing a symbol of courage and protection. As they searched for this symbol, these heroes met challenges, and as they developed courage, they overcame obstacles. Tiffany's coping strategies were then used to deal with parts of herself that had been blocked by a set of unrelenting standards that had been imposed by her parents. Her response to the problem was to avoid and withdraw. She retreated to the better and less restrictive worlds of her novels. When these were taken away from her by her father, she was left with little solace. Her negative behaviors exacerbated. She moved from withdrawal and reading, to withdrawal and nonperformance in school. Some youngsters respond to similar situations by withdrawing into emotion-focused coping that is often detrimental to their psychological development. It can be very difficult to help such youngsters find their way out of their withdrawn realities. One approach to this involves actually entering with them into a world that is withdrawn and different. For Tiffany, the entrance to this world was the opening of a cave. This fictive world was different in space and time but more controllable and therefore less frightening.

Fiction can be an escape from reality, but it can also be a way of dealing with covert issues, learning new strategies, and taking risks in a protected environment (Pehrsson, 2007). A counselor can uncover much about a client's story by creating an alternative but parallel story through the use of Co-story-ing. A youngster can also learn from the consequences—either good or bad—in self-controlled fiction. Using a narrative approach such as LFA can provide an exciting experience that parallels but also differs from the child's own living story. In such a story, the child encounters challenges and even danger while knowing he or she is safe. From dangerous yet safe excitement, humans can learn quickly and develop strategies that are long lasting. Such dangerous and safe experiences can be transformative, and the coping strategies developed within fiction can cross over into reality. When the group process is introduced, the benefits are enhanced.

Preadolescent youngsters, who are somewhat verbal, gain from strategies that engage their imaginations, provide for safe exploration of ideas and feelings, and allow for verbal expression that is less threatening than in traditional interventions.

child-centered
play counseling

Children play. They want to play almost all the time, but more than that they need to play almost all the time. It's their job, and they do it spontaneously, with boundless energy and total abandon. Play is a natural need for children because it is purposeful. Through play children learn about their worlds, relate actions to language, and gain mastery over fears and painful life circumstances. They prepare for later stages in their lives by role playing life skills. Children learn to be creative and resourceful in solving problems, identifying their own feelings and the feelings of others, making choices, and being responsible for these choices. They learn self-control, self-respect, and respect for others. They express themselves freely and become more self-directive. They become brave and sure. Through play, children also let counselors know about their desires, wishes, hopes, and dreams (Pehrsson & Aguilera, 2007). Most important, children demonstrate their coping behaviors, be they problem focused or emotion focused (see Chapter 2). They also express their core issue(s), which can be evidenced by their play with dolls or action figures and their interactions with the counselor. Behaviors in a play setting can expose maladaptive relational schemas in a manner not possible through traditional verbal-based interventions.

Play can be used to help children understand their perspectives, behaviors, feelings, and thoughts (Ablon, 1996; Landreth, 1991; O'Connor, 2000; Orton, 1996). Many helping professionals use play within the context of the therapeutic session to establish rapport, to engage children, and to provide children with a way of expressing themselves that does not rely on receptive or expressive verbal skills beyond the child's developmental level (Ablon, 1996). Play therapy techniques differ from traditional verbal-based counseling and therapy strategies. In play therapy, the helping professional relies on the child's play rather than his or her verbal responses as the communicative medium. Ginott (1961) recognized the parallel between language and play. He stated that play is a child's way of talking, and toys are the words. Children use play as one means of communicating their experiences (Axline, 1969; Landreth, 1991; Moustakas, 1953). The therapist who uses play therapy believes that children can communicate about their experiences through play. Engaging in play therapy allows children to tell their stories and gives the therapist the opportunity to hear them. The concept of working in a therapeutic relationship in which children are allowed to play out their feelings, thoughts, and experiences is fundamental to the play therapist no matter his or her theoretical orientation.

As noted previously, children differ from adults developmentally, cognitively, emotionally, physically, and psychologically. These differences require counselors who work with children to have specialized knowledge. Those who use play practices in counseling provide a therapeutic theater in which children can tell their stories. Children tell their core issues stories through their actions far better than they could through language alone. Because play therapy is not a form of talk therapy, one of the main tasks of the counselor is to observe quietly—at least, mostly quietly. Counselors need to be fully present, observe, and listen with their entire bodies (Pehrsson & Hoskins, 2009). Talk therapies can intimidate children, shut them down, and make the counseling relationship tenuous. The talkative counselor would do well to quiet down and not interrupt the child's play. Counselors should choose their reflections and responses carefully. In this chapter we suggest methods for the appropriate application of response phrases.

The Beginnings of Play Therapy Practices

Child-centered counseling is an outgrowth of person-centered theory as developed by Carl Rogers (1951). Person-centered counseling and child-centered counseling share the same basic philosophy of not depending on a series of techniques or procedures. Rather, they are ways of being.

The origin of child-centered play counseling (CCPC) was in the work of Virginia Axline (1947). A student of Carl Rogers, Axline drew from Rogers's research and applied his person-centered approach to work with children. The following quote captures how child-centered counseling was initially framed:

> Play therapy is based upon the fact that play is the child's natural medium for self expression. It is an opportunity which is given to the child to "play out" his feelings and problems just as, in certain types of adult therapy, an individual "talks out" his difficulties. (Axline, 1947, p. 9)

It is the relationship between the child and therapist—not the play itself—that supports the healing work in counseling (Axline, 1947). Like other theoretical approaches to play therapy, child-centered counseling incorporates a developmental perspective for approaching and understanding child clients (Axline, 1969; Kottman, 1999; Landreth, 1991; O'Connor, 2000; Rudolph & Thompson, 2000).

The child-centered approach to counseling asserts that children will heal, grow, and change if they are provided with an atmosphere in which the prosocial aspects of the self can flourish. The child-centered play counselor creates an atmosphere in which trust and acceptance are relayed, accurate empathic understanding is communicated, and the child's actions are valued. Two compatible philosophies, phenomenology and humanism, guide the approaches used in CCPC. The counselor adopts a phenomenological attitude by attempting to view the world from the child's frame of reference (Killough-McGuire & McGuire, 2001). The counselor also takes a stance that emphasizes the belief that humans strive toward self-actualization.

Rogers's person-centered approach to counseling is rooted in the confidence that the client has an innate motivation for positive growth or self-actualization. However, there are barriers to that growth, and the counselor's primary task is to facilitate the client's removing those obstacles to self-actualization. As the counselor establishes a nonthreatening environment that includes his or her positive and unconditional regard, the client increasingly feels safe and free to work through issues and to remove the barriers to self-actualization. Rogers's approach is a form of talk therapy and therefore differs from play therapy, which involves action with minimal talk. However, one of the major applications of Rogers's approach to play therapy is the role of the counselor as a facilitator and as the provider of a safe environment. This involves unconditional positive regard for the client and a set of four key beliefs that are centered on a deep respect for the client's innate motivation for self-growth. Rogers (1951, 1961) espoused four beliefs that are particularly applicable to CCPC: (a) People are trustworthy, (b) people move toward self-actualization, (c) people have their own resources for achieving their goals, and (d) people respond to their world based on their own unique interpretations of that world.

Axline (1969) applied Rogers's theory to developing an approach involving play interventions that also included cognitive and developmental constructs. A counselor who uses CCPC accepts the child unconditionally and establishes a permissive environment. However, limit setting is also important, as is discussed at great length later in this chapter. The counselor reflects activities without trying to interpret the child's meaning. Examples of how to implement this special form of communication also follow later in this chapter. Play therapy is a form of counseling primarily used with children ages 2 through 12. Although play has been adapted as a counseling technique in other theoretical frameworks, we believe that CCPC is the most beneficial framework and can form the basis of all counseling work with children. The counselor who follows this approach trusts children's ability to express their feelings through their interactions during play, and through this approach children can release fears and gain insight into their behavior and their core issues. The counselor who uses

CCPC is nondirective and thus allows the children themselves to come to realizations and insights that are developmentally appropriate. One premise for using CCPC is understanding that children are children, not miniature adults. The counselor encourages children to make their own choices and to realize the consequences of those choices. This attitude conveys a deep respect for children and for their abilities to solve their own problems or at least to reduce their anxieties. Children come to recognize that they themselves know which behaviors are most appropriate and which changes are most beneficial. The counselor knows that this is a gradual process and that children must lead and the counselor must follow. However, following does involve setting limits on behaviors that are inappropriate or perhaps dangerous in the play environment.

Although young children care deeply and have a wide range of emotional experiences and responses, they seldom have the verbal repertoire for expressing complex feelings. Children express feelings and concerns more effectively through actions than they do through language. Not only are children different from adults, but each child is unique and distinct from any other child. However, we believe that all children are able to survive, demonstrate resilience, and move toward what they need in the counseling process. This belief demonstrates respect. Counselors who use CCPC believe in children's capacity for growth and change. Counselors are patient and do not rush the process. They are comfortable with therapeutic silence and with waiting for a child's response. Within the context of CCPC, counselors promote situations in which children can make choices, show self-direction, have consistency, and use play, their most natural mode of communication, to express their feelings and concerns. Counselors believe that children will take what they need from the counseling process. They are comfortable with letting the child lead while they follow (Landreth, 2002a).

The counselor who uses a child-centered play intervention is able to create a safe and permissive atmosphere by embracing the child-centered philosophy and using the basic skills of tracking, reflection of feeling, limit setting, and redirection. These skills are adapted for the child's developmental level and overall functioning. The child is the leader and decides what and how to play. The child's play is tracked (e.g., "You decided to use the blocks") and his or her feelings reflected (e.g., "It's disappointing when they fall down"). Limit setting, recognition of feelings, and redirection are used if the play process becomes unsafe for either the child or play therapist (e.g., "In this room the blocks are not for throwing. I see you are angry and want to throw something. You can throw the squishy ball"). In this context, children can discover and experience aspects of the self while guiding the counselor on a journey of healing and growth.

CCPC Themes and Core Issues

Children tell their stories in play. As addressed in previous chapters, these stories or narratives are a living reflection of how children have constructed personal truths about themselves, others, and manner in which the world works. Children reveal their worries and wants in the form of allegories or metaphors, but they most often represent a reality that reflects their state of being. These stories often develop into a collective theme as children act, and over time various metaphors, symbols, styles, and rituals emerge. The astute counselor notices that core issue themes are often repeated in a variety of ways. A core issue theme may be presented as many as four to eight times per session, week after week. Themes may reappear from session to session. Some themes disappear suddenly or fade over time; some are replaced by new themes that gradually develop and evolve. The counselor recognizes, connects, and generalizes the individual play routines into themes. These themes provide data that allow the counselor to continually assess the nature of the child's expressed core issues. The counselor also recognizes growth and mastery as the child moves through the introduction stage of counseling toward establishing a therapeutic alliance and moving toward growth and healing. The counselor assesses by observing the child's play and by generalizing activities not as isolated actions but as representations of consistent personal truth themes underlying patterns of behavior (Halstead, 2007).

Counselors understand that such themes are windows into children's coping mechanisms and that children's thematic play connects to their lives outside the playroom. Patterns and themes that often emerge during CCPC include groupings of play activities related to power/control, nurturing/healing, boundary/intrusion, violation/protection, anger/ sadness, loyalty/betrayal, adjustment/change, self-confidence/cultural worth, identity, fear/anxiety, rejection/abandonment, security/trust, relationships/family, loss/death, and loneliness. By reading the child's "story," the counselor assesses the child's progress and determines when the child is ready to begin termination. The case of Cassie illustrates how core issue themes emerge when a child-centered play approach to counseling is used as the primary intervention.

The Case of Cassie

First Meeting

Cassie, a 4-year-old, entered the waiting room of the counselor's office clutching her Barbie doll and looking down at the floor. She found a small chair, huddled in it, and covered herself with throw pillows. The counselor, Nancy Jo, bent down and said, "You must be Cassie. I'm Nancy Jo. It is nice to meet you." Cassie barely peeked out from under the pillows and said a muffled, "'lo."

Cassie's mother, Terri Lee, had been referred by Child Protective Services and also by the pediatrician of their rural town. Nancy Jo specialized in working with children who experienced family dissolution and was well known for her positive results using play counseling.

Prior to their first meeting, Terri Lee had talked with Nancy Jo on the phone and had given her some background information. Although Terri

Lee and Cassie's father, Paul, had never married, they had lived together for 3 years. However, by the time Cassie had arrived Terri Lee and Paul had been growing apart. The relationship ended and Paul moved out after Cassie's third birthday. According to Terri Lee, the breakup was "nasty." However, Paul did retain visitation rights. Cassie slept over twice a month, every other Saturday night, at her father's house.

Terri Lee stated that about a year ago Cassie had begun having nightmares. Cassie told her mother, "A man came out of the closet. He was scary and he wanted to hurt me." The dream was repeated with variations. One time it was a monster climbing through her window, and another time she dreamed that she was in a store and a man jumped out and frightened her. After several nights of such dreams Cassie refused to go to bed. Terri Lee had told Nancy Jo that she thought there was a pattern: The dreams seemed to occur a few nights prior to Cassie visiting her father. Cassie became increasingly shy and started to withdraw from even her friends at nursery school. Her teacher reported that Cassie had hit and tried to bite another little girl who was just trying to be friendly. Terri Lee wanted to support Cassie's visits with her father but was becoming increasingly anxious about Cassie's behavior and thought there was a connection. On one occasion when Paul had beeped his car horn as a signal for Cassie to come to the car, Cassie had run into her mother's bedroom, hid under her bed, and cried, "I want to stay here!" She had then grabbed pillows from the bed and attempted to cover her stomach. Terri Lee had added, "After an investigation by Child Protective Services, Paul's brother was charged with crimes related to child pornography and lewd behaviors with a minor. I suspect he inappropriately touched Cassie when she was visiting Paul. I don't think it really was her stomach she was trying to cover and perhaps protect."

Nancy Jo thought that Cassie's situation had apparently been very negative and that she had tried to cope by removing herself from it. Cassie had tried to change her negative situation by avoiding visits to her father's house, where her Uncle Billy visited. But neither her father nor her mother understood the cause of her fears, and Cassie did not have the means to explain them. When this problem-focused coping did not work, Cassie developed emotion-focused coping strategies. These strategies relied on psychological processes such as nightmares and other expressions of fears. However, neither set of coping strategies had been successful at relieving her stress.

Nancy Jo considered Cassie's negative situation and her coping strategies along with the information provided by Cassie's mother. Based on the stressor threat model of coping (see Chapter 2), Nancy Jo understood that each child possesses sets of goals, beliefs, and knowledge that come together to form the basic nature of that individual. It would be very important that Cassie not alter her basic nature as a result of negative experiences. A successful outcome in Cassie's case would be to help her relieve her anxiety and learn to once again trust herself and others to avoid falling victim to a mistrust/abuse core issue.

Nancy Jo also understood the vital nature of this first counseling session in alleviating Cassie's fears. Nancy Jo continued to bend low as she talked softly to Cassie. She said, "I know you are curious about the playroom and about me. I'd like you and your mom to see where I work with children." She slowly stood up and said, "The playroom is right down the hall. Let's go take a look at it together."

Nancy Jo motioned to Terri Lee and Cassie, inviting them to walk with her. Cassie held back; she wasn't so sure. But as the adults wandered toward the playroom, Cassie soon fell into step, looking bright eyed as Nancy Jo turned on the lights. Cassie looked around at all of the toys and bright colors as if she had never seen a room like this in her whole life. Toys were neatly stacked on shelves so that a 4-year-old could reach all of them without any help.

Nancy Jo said, "This is where I work with children, and sometimes parents get to come in here and work, too. You look like you want to touch something but you are not sure. That is okay. In this room most everything is for touching."

Cassie shrugged, but Terri Lee picked up a cuddly puppet and said, "This is so cute! Cassie, look at this bear." Cassie shrugged again.

Nancy Jo walked past every shelf and talked about all of the toys on each shelf. By modeling, she demonstrated to Cassie that it was permissible to play with, touch, or pick up everything. Cassie lagged behind, but out of the corner of her eye Nancy Jo saw Cassie rubbing her shoulders against the shelves, her hands gently brushing against the dollhouse furniture. Nancy Jo sat on a child-size chair, beckoned her two guests to sit, and said, "Let me tell you a little more about our work together in the playroom."

Talking About the Work and the Tools of the Playroom

Nancy Jo talked about the ways in which she and children worked in the playroom. She explained that the playroom was a place where children could work out their worries. While Nancy Jo talked, Cassie's eyes searched the room. She saw a big wooden dollhouse with small dolls representing every age; some dolls were deep brown, some more golden, and some deep beige or light ivory. There were little beds, chairs, and even toilets for the dollhouse. Cassie's attention was drawn by the bright paints in the art corner. The shelves were filled with play dough, an easel with paints, crayons, markers, colored pencils, scissors, glue, and all kinds of colorful paper. She even saw a smock. She glanced beyond the paints and saw a little theater with curtains, and next to that was a shelf filled with puppets, dress-up clothes, and masks. Cassie smiled. She looked longingly at the puppets, but she sat still.

She looked over and saw a little kitchen stove, a sink, and a little table with chairs. She saw pots, pans, dishes, utensils, and miniature boxes of recognizable brands of food. There on the table sat a little teapot. She pointed to it and said, "Look, Mommy, the teapot is just like the one we have at home." Cassie seemed to say with her eyes and her smile, "This is okay. I could play here."

As she glanced away from the kitchen, she noticed large foam-covered blocks neatly stacked in a corner. Next to the blocks she saw cars, planes, trains, and a medical kit. She looked at one shelf and saw a big doll but frowned as if she was not sure she liked that toy. She saw a big bop bag that Nancy Jo called "Bo Bo." Cassie walked over to it with her right fist clenched as if she wanted to hit it, but then her hand relaxed and she backed away. Cassie looked around the room, taking it all in. Toys were everywhere, and it looked like they were laid out especially for her.

Nancy Jo was observing Cassie's eyes as they focused on different toys in the playroom. She could see that Cassie was engaged, interested, and ready for action. Nancy Jo had deliberately chosen her tools for the playroom so that a child like Cassie could play out his or her themes and worries without having labels preimposed upon them. The toys were as generic and simple as could be. Nancy Jo had chosen soft-edge furniture and shelves, and everything was child size. Nancy Jo had made sure her playroom contained materials that would support catharsis and emotional expression (such as wooden hammers for slamming, newspaper for ripping, and, of course, Bo Bo for whacking). She had gradually added creative and artistic materials such as play dough, clay, poster paints and fingerpaints, construction paper, scissors, and glue for children to represent their meanings and moods. Nancy Jo also had puppets and dress-up clothes, masks, hats, and sunglasses for drama play. She also included medical kits, a dollhouse, cars, planes, and kitchen and school supplies so that children could role play and act out real-life concerns. She had blocks, a sandbox, and building tools for construction projects. There were soft and cuddly materials for regression and for soothing needs. Toys were actually tools for children to use to play out their themes. As she had organized her room, Nancy Jo kept in mind that her tools (i.e., the toys) should promote a positive relationship, help children express a wide range of feelings, and assist children in exploring real-life experiences. She also knew that these tools should allow for testing of limits and aid in developing a positive self-image, self-understanding, and self-control. And of course, the room was soundproofed to maintain confidentiality.

Eighth Meeting: Cassie Tests the Limits

Nancy Jo and Cassie had been meeting weekly for almost 2 months when Cassie's themes began to shift. At the end of the eighth session the theme of her struggle became focused. Cassie had named one of the puppets "The Scary Guy," and at the beginning of each of the past three sessions she had grabbed The Scary Guy off the shelf and placed him in a large box in the left corner of the room. She had then put the lid on the box and covered it with toys. During the eighth session, Cassie's actions accelerated. She moved quickly and seemed to be searching for something she could not find. She sighed deeply and, looking at the door, announced, "I'm going to go now." This was quite unusual, for getting Cassie to stay in the playroom had never been a problem. Just the opposite, she was very reluctant to leave at the end of her sessions.

Nancy Jo, anticipating a hasty exit, moved toward the door and responded, "I know you feel like you need to go now, but we have ten more minutes together in the playroom."

Cassie looked—even glared—at Nancy Jo and stated, "I'm leaving now."

Undaunted, Nancy Jo calmly but firmly stood in front of the door and said, "It feels like time to leave, but we have a little more time. You get to decide what to do with our time." Nancy Jo used her hands to redirect Cassie's attention to the rest of the room. Cassie turned and looked around the room. Her eyes rested on the pile of blocks in the right corner. Nancy Jo reflected, "Looks like you have an idea."

With surefootedness, Cassie stomped over to the corner. She passed by the blocks and grabbed a police cap, which she plunked on her head. She reached up and pulled the cap down for a firm fit. Cassie then walked, as if marching, toward the blocks. She grabbed three of the largest blocks. She then marched to the box that held The Scary Guy and slammed the blocks on top of the box. She marched back to the pile of blocks, grabbed as many as she could carry, and piled block upon block on top of the box. When the top of the box was completely covered with a pile of blocks, Cassie folded her arms and exclaimed, "Now we are safe!"

Limit Setting

CCPC has four stages: introduction (getting to know one another), building a therapeutic alliance (building trust), growth (coming to terms with issues), and termination (ending the therapeutic relationship at the right time). Throughout these stages, the counselor encourages the child to make choices and to feel the freedom and safety to try out new behaviors. When children are offered choices, they have opportunities to learn self-control, to take responsibility for their own behavior, and to learn about themselves and their own well-being. A phrase that a counselor repeats often is "You get to choose." However, there are limits to children's choices. Limits provide physical and emotional security and safety for children, for they protect the physical well-being of the therapist and facilitate acceptance of the child. Limits anchor the session to reality and emphasize the here and now. Limits promote consistency in the playroom environment and protect the play therapy materials and room. Although the counselor establishes an environment of freedom and permissiveness, setting limits is an important part of the therapeutic process. Limit setting, which occurs throughout all stages of therapy, is foundational to developing trust and establishing a therapeutic alliance. Limits help keep relationships professional, ethical, and socially acceptable. Limits create consistency; therefore, the child learns to trust the counselor. Furthermore, limit setting connects the playroom with the reality of the world: The world has limits, and so does the playroom. Limits provide structure to the play counseling session and help clarify the nature of the therapeutic relationship.

Yet children get to choose within these limits. The limits are set by the counselor and may include what is best and appropriate for the therapeutic process. For example, during the eighth session Cassie chose to leave 10 minutes early. However, Nancy Jo limited Cassie's choices by firmly standing in front of the door and by redirecting Cassie to choose what to do with the remaining 10 minutes. Had Cassie left the room prematurely, she would not have had the opportunity to confront her fears and to master her anxiety related to The Scary Guy. By limiting Cassie's choice of leaving but also by redirecting her choices within the playroom, Nancy Jo acted appropriately.

Two guiding principles of limit setting serve well when one is working with children: Limits should be enforceable and as minimal as is reasonably possible. The child should never be read or told a long list of rules. Such a classroomlike activity is not appropriate in a counseling situation. Indeed, it would do damage during all four stages of CCPC. Reading rules is certainly no way to introduce unconditional positive regard. Limit setting occurs as the need arises, and when it does, counselors state limits in a very calm, patient, firm, and consistent manner. Providing limits during the first session is usually unnecessary. Just say, "There are a few things you need to know about how we work in the playroom. When you need to know something, I will tell you." The best time for a limit to be presented is when the issue arises during the session. When setting limits, play therapists acknowledge the child's wants, wishes, and feelings. They communicate the limit, reflect the feeling, and then target acceptable alternatives. For example, dragons and monsters may be killed in the playroom, but violence that would harm a person is not acceptable. If a child were about to hit the counselor, the counselor may make a defensive motion and state, "I'm not for hitting."

The counselor should always keep the focus of CCPC on the child in order to convey clearly where responsibility lies. Limit setting need not promote anxiety but can help in the development of trust. Counselors set reasonable consequences for noncompliance. A counselor can simply and firmly state, "It looks like you want to stay in the room, but our time is up today. Do you want to open the door or should I open the door?" If the child refuses to make a choice, after an appropriate period of waiting the counselor simply says, "It looks like you decided I get to open the door today." And the counselor surely and steadily walks toward the playroom door with hand extended to pull the doorknob. According to Landreth (2002a), when a child refuses to choose, the counselor chooses for the child. Choosing not to choose can be framed as a choice in itself: "Looks like you have decided I get to choose this time."

Saying Good-bye in the Playroom

In CCPC, termination is a critical stage. The counselor plans for this stage from the first session. Ordinarily the number of sessions is predictable, very often planned more by the insurance company than by anything else. However, terminations can be abrupt. Almost all private practitioners have heard a variation of this phrase: "I checked with my insurance company.

Today has to be Jonna's last session." A sudden termination may result from the family moving out of the area. Caregivers can and sometimes do remove a child with little or no notice. Counselors do what they can to terminate a therapeutic relationship with a child and not add to the emotional baggage that child might have. But there are guidelines to follow and respectful ways of saying good-bye.

It is hoped that as the counselor moves toward ending work with a child, the child has moved through each stage of CCPC and has learned valuable skills. Several questions guide the counselor in determining when termination should occur. Nancy Jo's decision to terminate Cassie's sessions was based on positive changes in the child's behaviors that Cassie's mother had reported and that she herself had observed. Cassie had become less dependent and less needy both in the playroom and with family and friends. She had become friendlier at school. She helped clean up the playroom at the end of sessions. She no longer feared visiting her father and even told her mother about the adventures she had on such weekends. Most of all, she became her own young person who was willing to try new experiences.

Children themselves may indicate that they are ready to terminate. A child may demonstrate such feelings regarding termination symbolically. For example, one indication may be a drawing of bridges. This may show that the child is ready to cross that bridge to the other side by themselves. Whatever the sign, children are smart, and they know what termination means when it is explained and the process worked through. This can be a tough time for children as well as a time to celebrate. But it is important to take the time to make it what it needs to be for each child.

Counselors can introduce closure with objects such as a bridge or through drawing. It is useful to remind the child at each session how many more times you both will be working together. Children have varying abilities to comprehend time and space, and counselors need to consider their developmental and cognitive abilities.

When the last session finally arrives, the counselor can direct the closing time through many different play techniques. For example, make a paper basket. As both you and the child put little chocolates or candies inside, tell each other a memory of your work together. Children also like rituals such as having a tea party. Some like to sing songs, eat popcorn, or make a good-bye picture. Sometimes children will bring a small present from home. It is important to talk to parents about this beforehand. An expensive gift should usually be discouraged. However, a handmade gift or card is just what the child may need to create to honor the process. Some counselors make a symbolic timeline or a "calendar" and have the child remember what was done throughout the weeks in counseling. (This is particularly appropriate for older children.)

Children may experience different feelings when termination is near. Old themes or feelings of abandonment, loss, loneliness, anxiety, and being punished may temporarily resurface. Yet good themes may emerge as well: a sense of joy with accomplishment and success, happiness, pride, and autonomy.

For her last session, Cassie chose to have a tea party. She looked up at Nancy Jo and said, "More tea?"

Nancy Jo nodded, smiled, and said, "I remember how quiet you were the first time you came in this room. Now you are sure and brave."

Cassie said, "Nancy Jo, how come you never help me?"

Nancy paused and quietly said, "That is because you can do many things all by yourself. In this room you got to decide what you could do."

Cassie looked at Nancy Jo and proclaimed, "That's right, I can do a lot of things. I can do them all by myself."

Summary

When paired with the concepts of core issue themes, child-centered counseling can be a very useful approach to understanding the struggles children experience. Providing multiple play modalities enables the child's world to emerge and provides an opportunity for the counselor to join the child in finding new and adaptive mechanisms for coping and creating change.

chapter 8

sand work in counseling and connecting with children's core issues

This chapter addresses the process of engaging children in working with their core issues through the use of the sand tray. Two different cases are presented as a means of illustrating clinically effective models of intervention. In one the counselor helps a young girl process her anger, and in the other this intervention is used to help a child develop stronger and more adaptive coping strategies.

The Case of Kazzie

Kazzie fondled the sand with her hands. Her eyes were calm now. A soft smile played on her lips, almost resting there as she stretched her hands and buried them into the sandbox. She sighed deeply, her shoulders dropped, and she removed her hands. Kazzie gently picked up the figure of a dog from atop the sand mound and held it in her hands with care. She looked up, and her eyes searched the middle shelf. Without missing a beat, she reached up and took a small golden box from the shelf. She placed the figure in the box and covered it with the lid. Slowly, with deliberate purpose, she dug a second small hole in the sand and placed the box in it. Kazzie carefully spread the sand until the box was covered and gone from view. She stopped, breathed deeply, and whispered something inaudible. Kazzie's eyes searched the shelf and focused sequentially on a Star of David, a small heart, three rhinestones, and a miniature dog bone. Tenderly, Kazzie placed all four items on the grave. She looked up at Ms. Sandler and said, "I am done now. Mr. Jax is sleeping and dreaming good things." This was Kazzie's second sand tray funeral of the day.

Sand Work Premises

Counseling children with sand work provides a kinesthetic method that literally grounds children to the issues at hand. When children place both hands in the sand, their responses may vary, but each response is meaningful (Homeyer & Sweeney, 2005). The process may energize or relax, create awe or disgust; however, the response is never neutral. Like play counseling, sand tray work provides a physical medium for children to act out themes and relevant concerns occurring in their lives. Children are action creatures. They have a need to express themselves, and they often express themselves best in modes other than verbal ones. The sand tray provides a container and a therapeutic setting—a stage—for children to express feelings and even to explain their core issues to counselors, who are able to interpret a sort of language of actions.

Although sand work is often used with children, it is appropriate for use with people of all ages because the activity naturally adapts to any developmental stage. Sand work is particularly appropriate for use with children ages 7 through 18 years of age. However, we concentrate here on younger children, for whom it is obvious that sand work produces positive therapeutic outcomes. Many play therapists suggest including a sandbox in the playroom, and many experts in child counseling recommend it as a core piece of equipment (Homeyer & Sweeney, 1998, 2005; Landreth, 2002a; Oaklander, 1988). Sand work has many advantages. The sand itself is soothing and prompts relaxation. As children run their hands through the sand, counselors observe the soothing physical responses that emerge: the restful stroking of the arm, the breathing that slows and becomes deeper, and often the calm smile that rests on the child's face. The kinesthetic quality of sand provides the tactile learning and sensation children need. It allows for exploration and discovery when children bury ordinary objects but then uncover hidden secrets and unearth solutions from the sand. Sand work presents opportunities for the release of emotions and allows for cathartic expression (Lowenfeld, 1993). With their hands in the sand, children can use objects to control anxiety, master fearful events, and conquer fears. For those children who are afraid to "get messy" lest they "get in trouble," sand work provides for a corrective behavioral experience and risk taking in the "dirt." Children can practice real-life skills and replay real-life events in the sand. Sand produces glee and freedom. It also provides opportunities for the counselor to work with children on limit setting and boundaries (Boik & Goodwin, 2000; De Domenico, 1998; Homeyer & Sweeney, 2005).

Many who support the use of sand work in counseling argue that sand has archetypal qualities, especially if used in conjunction with water (Cunningham, 2003; Kalff, 1980; Preston-Dillon, 1999). Most proponents agree that sand work deeply touches the psyche (Lowenfeld, 1946, 1950, 1960; Turner, 2005). Sand can symbolize many things, including the earth, rebirth, and death; water can symbolize cleansing. Children can use sand to make tunnels; model hiding, drowning, burials, or earthly disasters; and act out many other emotional metaphors. The sand tray itself sets limits and provides a safety zone. The sand tray is the setting, a sort of stage, for children to play out meaningful happenings in their lives (Kalff, 1980).

The sand tray itself is the vehicle or the major therapeutic tool used during the session. The work in the sand is called *sand work* or *sandplay*. The *sand world* is the product that is created (Homeyer & Sweeney, 1998; Turner, 2005). Counselors who use sand tray or sand work understand the power and healing that can occur with appropriate use. Sand work is often seen as a creative and expressive mode of counseling. It offers opportunities for a child to externalize and to project onto the sand hidden concerns and unconscious feelings. Sand work as a counseling modality involves the discovery and processing of intra- and interpersonal core issues expressed primarily nonverbally. The process is initiated by the client yet guided by the counselor (Cunningham, 1997, 2003).

Although the benefits are similar, counseling children with sand work is different from using a sandbox in play therapy or child-centered play counseling. A small sandbox may be included along with other materials in play counseling, but sand work requires a stand-alone sand tray and unique tools and involves a specific type of intervention within a separate work area. Kalff (1980) recommended that the tray be a rectangular box, approximately 28 to 29 inches by about 20 inches and 3 inches deep. We suggest using white, soft, garden sand, which is best for texture and movement and is easily brushed off the hands. The base and sides of the sand tray are usually painted blue (as a metaphor for water or the sky), and wood is preferred, as it is a natural and warm material. As recommended by Homeyer and Sweeney (1998), the sand tray should sit solidly on a table situated where students can access it either by standing or, if they choose, by sitting on a stool. The counselor amasses an extensive collection of small figurines that are placed on shelves (usually arranged thematically) and that are visually and physically available to clients (Preston-Dillon, 2007; Turner, 2005).

Sand Work Benefits

Sand work has many benefits, especially for children who lack verbal fluency. Sand work is an especially effective and efficient mode of communication for clients with delayed development or impaired verbal communication skills.

Sand work promotes the expression of nonverbalized issues and feelings and thus allows children to connect their feelings with their experiences. The kinesthetic quality of the sand is unique in the therapeutic process, and its tactile quality can provide relief from distress. Just by providing sand work as a focal process the counselor can help children access core issues. The sand creates an often necessary therapeutic distance for clients as it becomes a safe place for abreaction to occur. Repressed issues can emerge, be relieved, and be resolved. Negative feelings can be expressed.

Sand provides a healing component and is effective in the treatment of trauma (Homeyer & Sweeney, 1998).

The use of the sand tray pushes boundaries and helps set limits within which the child gains a sense of control and consistency. The sand and the sand tray tools are a setting for the use of metaphors that represent relevant situations and issues in the world of the child. Sand work provides a representation that a client and counselor can use to discuss important matters. Working in the sand helps counselors to dispel client fears and overcome client resistance. Deeper intrapsychic issues may be addressed more rapidly, and complex issues may be approached more gently (Lowenfeld, 1993). Transference is often an issue in counseling, especially when verbal interactions focus on the relationship between the client and the counselor (Cunningham, 2003). However, in sand work the focus is on the interactions that are taking place in the sand tray, and this can reduce incidences of transference. Work in the sand challenges transference by creating an alternative object of focus that is not the counselor. And finally, the use of sand work can cut through verbalization used as a defense (Boik & Goodwin, 2000; Cunningham, 1997).

Engaging in sand tray work requires extensive education, training, and supervision. There are many resources for this training, including universities and workshops endorsed by the Association for Play Therapy and the Association for Sand Tray Therapy.

Historical Background

Victorian author and nontraditionalist thinker H. G. Wells authored a relatively obscure work related to children's (particularly his own son's) war games and play with miniature figures (Turner, 2004). Wells recognized the power of such play and shared his appreciation for the transformations he observed in his own child. His work related to games using miniatures was lighthearted and somewhat humorous; it posed questions and made suggestions regarding the nature, purpose, and methods of play using miniatures and other small props.

Wells's work inspired physician and child therapist B. Margaret Lowenfeld and facilitated her creation of the "World Technique," which she officially put forth in 1929 (Lowenfeld, 1946; Turner, 2004). Lowenfeld was multilingual and had served as an interpreter during World War I. She realized the potential for problems with misinterpretations and questioned the validity of language as the primary means of therapeutic intervention with children. She argued that other modes of communicating had stronger therapeutic effects. Lowenfeld added sand trays and water to her practice, and the sand tray work that is so valuable today was born. Lowenfeld also drew from her near contemporaries in the development of her play and sand techniques. Yet Lowenfeld herself claimed that her method emerged naturally from her work with children and credited the children themselves with having developed the technique. Melanie Klein, Donald Winnicott, and Ronald Fairbairn also influenced the development of sand work (Preston-Dillon, 2007; Turner, 2004, 2005).

Dora M. Kalff, a Swiss analyst, was encouraged by Carl Jung to study Lowenfeld's work. Kalff integrated Lowenfeld's techniques with her own Jungian and Christian–Tibetan Buddhist perspectives to develop an approach she named *sandplay therapy*. She understood sandplay to be a transpersonal methodology as well as a psychological one. Kalff went on to develop recommendations regarding the stance that a practitioner should take as well as the specific set of skills to use in sand work (Kalff, 1980; Lowenfeld, 1993; Turner, 2005).

Sandplay and sand work migrated from Europe to the United States in the 1950s. They have since expanded to include various theoretical frameworks and have been applied to diverse clinical populations. Some of the better known experts in sand work include Turner (2005), Homeyer and Sweeney (2005), Cunningham (2003), Boik and Goodwin (2000), Lowenfeld (1993), De Domenico (1988), and Kalff (1980). Sand work is known by several other clinical names, including *sandplay therapy*, *sand tray therapy*, *sand world play*, and *sand tray journeying*. No matter what it is called, sand work helps children understand their worlds and helps counselors better understand the experiences and needs of children. Sand work has particular utility in school settings: It provides an immediate conjoined focus and allows for counseling work to begin quickly as children are able to manipulate a miniature world they create (Turner, 2004).

Kazzie and the Loss of Mr. Jax

Kazzie, a 12-year-old sixth grader, was trying to make sense of her world after she witnessed the brutal murder of her dog, Mr. Jax. Seated in the back of the school bus, Kazzie had watched Mr. Jax run onto the side of the road and attempt to follow her. The driver of a car coming up behind the bus deliberately swerved to hit the dog. Mr. Jax was run over and lay lifeless in the road. Kazzie watched as the car passed the school bus. The young driver and three other boys in the car were laughing. By the time the bus arrived at school, Kazzie had been intermittently crying silently and screaming uncontrollably. After all of the other children had exited the bus, Kazzie remained frozen in her seat. The bus driver had observed the killing of the dog in the rearview mirror and understood Kazzie's deep hurt. He stopped the engine, exited the bus, and headed directly for Ms. Sandler, the school counselor, who was greeting children as they entered the building. She was able to talk Kazzie into coming to her office. She then called Kazzie's grandmother, with whom Kazzie lived, and informed her about Kazzie's grief. They agreed that it would be best for Kazzie to stay at school and to spend some time with Ms. Sandler. Kazzie was still sobbing as she walked into the counseling room. Her tears subsided as she gazed at the shelves and a large tray filled with sand.

Sand Work Room and Tools

Ms. Sandler's room, which had been converted from a special education classroom, had built-in wooden shelves that were narrow and nicely set for holding large sheets of paper. Some shelves were just perfect for her figurines, most of which were no higher than 4 inches. The wall immediately opposite the entrance rose to 10 feet in height and had shelves from the floor to the ceiling. When her student clients entered, they fully grasped the purpose of the room. Ms. Sandler wanted the room itself to speak of its purpose, and indeed it did. It said, "In this room you can work out worries using figures in the sand. In this room you can tell your story."

Ms. Sandler had planned her room specifically to meet the needs of her middle school clients. Most of the children in her school were 11 to 14 years old. They fluctuated between being childlike, playful, and ultra-cool. Sometimes they were cruel and sexually explorative, and on other occasions they just wanted to be coddled. They were 'tweens, and Ms. Sandler's counseling office was appropriately designed for this developmental stage. She had a pet hamster named Axie (for Virginia Axline), lots of games and interactive toys, and a corner sand work area that was appropriately named *Sand World* (but to herself she called it *Planet Dune*).

When Ms. Sandler welcomed students to her workroom, she often noted their looks of surprise. Some students might say, "What the heck is this with all the toys?" or "This is weird," or "I'm not touching those dolls." Others might say, "Cool dragons," or "I like your stuff. Is it okay to touch them?" Ms. Sandler responded softly, stating, "Sometimes people can't find the right words. These figures can help find them." She followed with, "If you would like to work in the sand today, we can do that." Reading a student's interested response and seeing wide-opened eyes that wanted more, she would guide the student around the room, explaining the way they might work together using the sandbox. Usually students walked over to the figurines with a hand extended, ignoring the sandbox. So Ms. Sandler would follow their cue and walk over to the shelf.

The shelves held about 200 figurines that she had collected from various toy stores, garage sales, and her favorite place, the local model railroad supply store. All her figurines, which she called her *tools*, were arranged thematically and had been deliberately chosen for the purpose of helping her clients play out needed themes and symbolize what was meaningful to them. She categorized them in certain ways, fully cognizant that clients draw different meanings from symbols and that representations are highly personal. She selected tools that could represent varied themes children might play out in the counseling process, such as conflict, aggression, anger, revenge, death, loss, abandonment, secrets, power, building, creation, transition, treasures, connection, relationships, loneliness, family, religion, spirituality, control, helplessness, depression, hurt, fear, safety, nurturance, healing, acceptance, and belonging.

With these specific themes in mind, Ms. Sandler chose her tools wisely. One shelf represented religion and spirituality. Some items included a Star of David, a hexagram, a cross, a small Buddha, an angel, a miniature dreamcatcher, a tiny Koran, a figure of Joseph Smith, and a statuette of Our Lady of Guadalupe. Each figurine was placed facing forward, lined up with just a small space separating it from its neighbor.

On the fantasy and mysticism shelf, Ms. Sandler had carefully placed moons, shining stars, magic wands, dark and light crystals, scary and kind wizards, prancing and proud unicorns, formidable gargoyles, witches with moles and witches with smiles, green trolls and winged fairies, fire-breathing dragons and their hatching eggs, and other mythical beasts.

On the people shelf stood curly haired tall and short folk, doll-like creatures with large bellies and round hips, people with smiles, some without, some sad, some angry, and some with emotions hard to read. Some figures were glazed with ebony, some tanned and olive, and others coated with ivory. Little versions of real people stood, clothed for play, fun, and all kinds of work. Some were not dressed at all. A little girl sat in her wheelchair reading a book. Some people stood erect, whereas others leaned on walkers or canes. Some wore speckled glasses, eye patches, or hearing aids; some were missing limbs. Characters were outfitted from countries and continents all over the globe.

Animals and insects from every climate lined the next shelf. There were zebras, gorillas, elephants, hummingbirds, giraffes, snakes, butterflies, snakes, spiders, bears, lions, tigers, alligators, foxes, squirrels, rabbits, wolves, eagles, and fish. Some appeared benign, but a few, such as the green monster with sharp teeth and the python coiled and ready to strike, provoked fear. Cows, sheep, pigs, chicks, and horses prompted some farmlike themes, and animals such as cats, dogs, ferrets, guinea pigs, and parrots rounded things out on the domestic front.

Vegetation and landscape materials lined one large shelf, providing opportunities for children to create their world, or at least their hopes of a world better than the one in which they currently lived. In neatly stacked columns stood plants, flowers, bushes, trees, pebbles, boulders, caves, mountains, rivers, streams, and small ponds.

One shelf contained building structures, transportation signs, cultural accessories, tools, representations of careers, creative symbols, and musical items. Ms. Sandler had walls, fences, gates, bricks, stairs, bridges, small buildings, cars, bikes, police and emergency vehicles, trains, boats, and planes. She had stop signs, warning signs, and stoplights. She had placed little trumpets, horns, drums, pianos, flutes, bells, and chimes on one shelf. She was careful to select items that were meaningful across cultures, and she updated her items to represent other cultures as needed. She understood that if she placed it on her shelf, she had to have a pretty good idea of what it might mean to her clients and the therapeutic power it might invoke.

The First Funeral

Kazzie looked around the room. With just a glance at Ms. Sandler, who nodded her acceptance, she walked over to the shelf with animals, selected a figure of a dog, and placed it in the center of the sand tray. Her tears streamed onto the sand and onto the dog. She took a car from a shelf and buried the car in the sand and placed the dog on top of the mound.

Kazzie wiped tears from her eyes, looked up at Ms. Sandler, and smiled slightly. Then she removed the dog from atop the car's grave and buried it. "I'm okay now. Can I go to my classroom?"

Ms. Sandler watched Kazzie walk down the hall and into her classroom. Then she looked at the sand tray and did what she usually did: She focused her digital camera and took a picture of it. At the end of the school day, after many other children had constructed their worlds in the sand tray, Ms. Sandler placed the photograph of Kazzie's sand world on her desk. She thought how Kazzie had changed a very negative situation by reframing the event. Kazzie had already begun to cope with a very noxious element in her environment. In instances such as this, in which the trauma cannot be undone, a child has no choice other than to respond by initiating emotion-focused coping strategies. Was this reframing a positive coping strategy? The first funeral, that of the car, certainly expressed Kazzie's anger—a justified anger—but in the burial of the dog Kazzie expressed the very sad reality of her trauma. Ms. Sandler whispered to herself, "I do hope this strategy is healthy. Time will tell."

Although she and Kazzie worked together just one time, Ms. Sandler continued to watch Kazzie from afar, and several times she checked with her teacher. She often greeted Kazzie, especially when she arrived at school. Kazzie had experienced a major trauma in her life, but she appeared to have started to heal, perhaps more quickly because, with the help of the sand tray, she represented the anger and grief of having lost her beloved Mr. Jax. If this were the case, this sad event involving Mr. Jax would not leave Kazzie with a lasting core issue of maladjustment. She would not generalize the action of one driver to mistrust the intentions of others in her life. Neither would she blame herself to the point of experiencing an unrelenting sense of defectiveness and shame over this loss. If no core issue became apparent over time this would be a very sad but thankfully isolated event in Kazzie's young life.

The next case study, that of Julia, presents a different challenge from the one Kazzie faced. Julia's struggle did not originate from the trauma of an isolated loss but rather from ongoing domestic hardship she endured for an extended period of time.

The Case of Julia

Julia stomped into the workroom. Her dark lined eyes glistened menacingly as she glanced up at the shelves and cracked her bubblegum. Although it was a warm day, Julia wore a sweater with long sleeves and was perspiring. Ms. Sandler wanted to ask Julia if she wanted to remove her sweater. But she thought better of it and decided to say nothing.

Ms. Williams, Julia's sixth-grade homeroom teacher, had referred Julia to Ms. Sandler for issues involving anger management. According to Ms. Williams's referral form, Julia was a "loner" and would threaten other children who approached her. She would often scream if anyone touched her, even by accident. Ms. Williams also stated that Julia almost always wore a long-sleeved shirt or sweater, but on a few occasions when she had seen Julia's arms, they had had scars and, a few times, open cuts.

To Ms. Sandler's surprise, Julia whispered politely, "Can I touch this stuff?"

Ms. Sandler nodded yes, "Yes you can."

Julia reached slowly for the fire-breathing dragon and the wizard and asked, "What do I do with these?"

Ms. Sandler explained, "In this room you can choose figures that seem important to you or maybe 'speak' to you by fitting into some kind of a story. You can use the figures to create a 'world' in the sand tray."

Julia sighed and looked at the shelf again. She slowly glanced from shelf to shelf, touching and pausing at certain figures and symbols but letting her hand drop away each and every time. Ms. Sandler waited and then spoke, "Julia, if you are willing, maybe you can create your world for me in the sand. What do you think?"

Julia answered, "I can try, but I don't want to talk today." Ms. Sandler explained that some days were just for working but not for talking, and that was okay too.

Julia instantly set to work. Then her body relaxed and gently, almost reverently, she picked up a small lamb and placed it in a corner of the sand tray. Her hands moved quickly and with assuredness, as if she had memorized all of the items on the shelf; she knew exactly where to reach and what to grab. Julia worked silently for 20 minutes until the entire sand tray was filled with more than 30 objects. The lamb was standing in the right corner behind rocks, walls, and fences Julia had placed in the sand. In front of the barriers Julia had sculpted riverbeds and mountains. Directly on the other side of the barriers a fire-breathing dragon and a wizard stood as if they were glaring at the lamb. Dark rocks, crystals, and spiders were cast about. A pile of polished stones was piled high and deliberately placed across the center of the tray. Julia stepped back and examined her work. She looked at Ms. Sandler squarely, exclaiming, "Well that's it! That's my world! I'm outta here! Later." And before Ms. Sandler could respond, the door to her office slammed shut and all that was left of Julia was the scent of her bubblegum.

Ms. Sandler looked down at the sand tray. Today it had been transformed into Julia's world. The tray itself seemed to speak or perhaps to scream. Ms. Sandler wanted to speak for the lamb. She whispered, "Keep away from me!"

Sand Worlds

Ms. Sandler thought about the many "worlds" that children had created during her years at Green Valley Middle School in southern Nevada. The children had offered many worlds for her to read and interpret. Some worlds seemed barren and empty, some fenced in and barrierlike, some heavily populated. Some were chaotic, whereas others were rigidly organized. Some were war zones. Today she was staring at Julia's world, an unpeopled, highly rigid world. Its predominant theme was that of barriers deliberately placed in front of the lamb. The lamb stood protected and blocked from the other animal figures. The stones, walls, and fences were methodically stacked and packed to prevent passage to either side.

Ms. Sandler hypothesized, "Julia is blocked too. Closed off from friends and family, much of her time is spent in angry outbursts that keep people from getting close. Then when her anxiety and loneliness become too much to bear, she inflicts small cuts on her arms that she then covers with long-sleeved shirts." She wondered whether the long sleeves Julia wore during the sweltering Nevada summer were at least partly responsible for her discomfort and sweat.

Ms. Sandler was well aware of specific guidelines for her sand work; she read extensively, attended many training sessions, and met with a monthly supervision group. Indeed, she often created her own tray as a response to her work with the children. She was sensitive to what the tray could tell her about her work with clients. She also realized that it was very possible to misinterpret a sand tray. Therefore, she would process her trays with her peers. Supervision also proved helpful in shedding light on the most challenging of cases (S. Cameron, 2003; Friedman & Mitchell, 2008).

Ms. Sandler thought about how each sand tray resulted in a sand world. She considered the Planet Dune part of her office unique. She was thinking about all of these things as she snapped a picture of Julia's world. She sighed. Gently and quietly she approached the tray, respecting the creation, for this was Julia's private, almost sacred space. She took several pictures of the tray from various angles, knowing that once she looked at them again, new insights and details would emerge. She stood where Julia had been and took several more pictures. During the session she would never have touched the contents or the tray itself, but now that Julia was gone, she slowly removed each figure and tool from the sand while monitoring her own feelings and thoughts. She was particularly struck by the weight she sensed when removing the walls and stones, so heavy. Rather than overanalyzing the content and product of the tray, Ms. Sandler took the stance of a spectator and honored without judgment the story that Julia had told her without any words.

During the session, both Ms. Sandler and Julia had been very quiet. Ms. Sandler had stood back to give Julia space, yet not so far away that Julia could not discern her supportive presence. Ms. Sander was struck by the energy that Julia had brought to the sand tray. Julia had moved quickly, with purpose, building high walls, using the full power of her arms, flexing muscles as she moved the sand, her feet almost mounted to the floor. Ms. Sandler had stood and observed as Julia had labored in the sand and had commented, "It looks like you know what you're doing."

During her second session Julia walked into the room and immediately took figures and other items off the shelf. She placed them in the sand and then stepped back and stood staring down at the sand tray. She had recreated more or less the same sand world as she had during her first visit. This time, however, she added another figurine: a bear sitting in the corner. One wall had a small cranny; otherwise, all barriers and walls were tightly stacked. Julia sighed deeply, "Now what?"

Ms. Sandler requested, "Tell me the name of this world you created."

Julia paused, her eyes taking in the wholeness of the tray. "The trap."

There are many ways in which counselors can process sand trays with their clients, and in our experience, children, even the most verbal, do not process the same way as adults. Their processing is usually short and brief, and the counselor keeps this in mind. Yet it is no less rich a therapeutic encounter. When processing sand trays with her student clients, Ms. Sandler followed an adaptation of the model recommended by Homeyer and Sweeney (1998, 2005). First she requested that the client title the work. She would not offer any choice in the matter. She knew from experience that if she asked children, "Do you want to give your world a name?" they would exclaim, "No!"

Once Julia named the tray, Ms. Sandler prompted her to discuss the whole tray, stating, "Tell me about this world named *The Trap*." She moved from the general picture to the specific discoveries, suggesting that Julia comment on the whole tray, including the sand mounds or "the walls." She then moved on to the specific elements, stating, "I noticed there is a bear in the corner." While she was processing the tray with Julia, Ms. Sandler examined the details and the process behind the tray. She noticed elements that stood out, noted which things surprised her, and looked for dominant patterns. Certainly, the walls, fences, and barriers formulated a pattern, but the newly added bear was a surprise. Ms. Sandler waited to ask about the bear, holding her curiosity in check. Ms. Sandler never asked the client, "Are you in this world?" She preferred to let that discovery unfold on its own, but even so she liked to guess which figure was the client. Sometimes a client might identify with more than one figure. Ms. Sandler looked at the dragon and the lamb and wondered if they represented two parts of Julia. She glanced around the tray, pondering which character had the most power and which the least, which the most energy and which the least.

Sometimes once the details of the tray were discussed, Ms. Sandler invited the client to ask the characters or the figures to speak, to feel, or to move around the tray. She always noted where the main characters were in relation to everything else. She observed the energy, movement, and behaviors behind the creation. Ms. Sandler always used her own reaction to the scene as a fairly reliable gauge as to what the child was expressing. She knew that when engaging a child in sand work, the counselor lets the client guide the process and uses counseling skills to understand the child's world.

When the session seemed complete, Ms. Sandler turned to Julia and asked, "Is there anything you would like to move, change, or add to the sand tray?"

Julia looked around the room and walked sure-footedly to the insect shelf, where she grabbed a butterfly. She placed it near the bear.

Ms. Sandler said, "Is there a new title for the world?"

Julia glanced sideways at Ms. Sandler and said, "Not today."

Later Ms. Sandler collapsed into her chair, absentmindedly stroking the stuffed bear that always sat here. She gazed at the sand tray and thought about what she had learned from Julia. It seemed to her that Julia was trying to protect herself from some situation. She had developed coping strategies, but they were not benefiting her. She was isolating herself, and this seemed to be represented by the lamb. As Ms. Sandler attempted to understand Julia better she said softly to herself, "But that butterfly! What about that butterfly? And that lamb? There is a soft side to Julia that she works to keep hidden. Perhaps she is now ready for it to be uncovered."

Supervision and the Peer Group

Ms. Sandler showed the photographs of Julia's two trays to her peer group of school counselors in her next supervisory session. These sessions involved case reviews and were conducted professionally and with strict confidentiality. Two of the counselors were aware of Julia's family. They reported that the family had experienced some traumatic events over the past 2 years. Julia's mother had turned to drinking after the death of her son in Iraq. After the departure of her husband and the subsequent divorce, things had gotten even worse. Julia lived with her mother, who had full parental custody. There were no other siblings. Julia's mother had refused help from the county social services agency and denied that she had problems.

After the session, and based on suggestions that had emerged from the group, Ms. Sandler started to develop a plan for helping Julia. She realized that Julia's mother's avoidance coping process included large amounts of alcohol and resulted in behaviors that were not conducive to helping Julia cope with a stressful situation. She understood that Julia was not able to change her negative situation, nor could she remove herself from the environment. Therefore, Julia had developed another means of coping with the noxious elements in her environment. Any effort on Julia's part to directly address and change her home condition would most likely fail and probably had in the past. Julia had most likely determined, whether consciously or not, that her resources for reducing or alleviating these stressors were inadequate. Therefore, she had activated emotion-focused coping resources in an attempt to minimize the effects of the threatening conditions. Ms. Sandler theorized that Julia had quickly learned that she could not trust her father or her mother. With the formation of a core issue of mistrust, and given the multiple environments in which it was triggered, Julia generalized her living story such that she came to trust no one. As Julia lived out her story she developed a self-protective and very negative set of coping behaviors. These coping behaviors included emotional and physical disengagement and the inappropriate venting of emotions with others. The results of these negative coping strategies were self-hatred and the inflicting of further harm by cutting her arms.

Keeping in mind the helpful suggestions from her peer supervisory group, Ms. Sandler developed a plan based on the theory that Julia had no chance of changing her home situation. When her problem-focused coping strategies had failed, Julia had activated negative emotion-focused coping mechanisms. Ms. Sandler planned how to help Julia form at least the beginning of a trusting relationship. Forming a relationship seemed to represent a basic step toward developing a more positive emotion-focused coping strategy and could mitigate the effects of the mistrust core issue.

When Julia arrived for the next session, Ms. Sandler said, "Today we are going to do something different. Bettina and Jollie are going to be here soon, and the three of you get to work in the sand tray." Julia was sitting in the corner of the room and immediately folded her arms when Bettina and Jollie arrived. When Bettina and Jollie saw Julia, they turned around and took two steps toward the door. It seemed apparent to Ms. Sandler that these girls were already acquainted with one another. Ms. Sandler convinced Bettina and Jollie that it would be safe to remain. However, the session was difficult. For the first 15 minutes Julia remained in the corner, sitting very still with her arms tightly folded. Her teeth were clenched, her face tight, and her eyes glared not at the sand tray but at the two other girls. Bettina and Jollie worked in the sand tray without saying a word. Each seemed to keep one eye on Julia.

After the girls had returned to their classrooms, Ms. Sandler took a picture of the sand tray and prepared the room for her next young client by replacing the figures on the shelves and smoothing the sand. Later that day, Ms. Sandler looked at the photo of the sand tray that Bettina and Jollie had constructed without help from Julia, who had spent the entire session sitting in the corner. They had placed their usual villain, Green Monster, in the center of the tray. Bettina had placed the figure of a woman holding a blanket on the right side of the tray, and Jollie had placed a girl figure on the left side. Jollie's figure was holding an umbrella.

Ms. Sandler had been working individually with both Bettina and Jollie for several months. They had also been referred for anger management and had worked out many of their core issues. For the past four sessions the two girls had worked together and had demonstrated a willingness to cooperate with each other; they even seemed to be building trust. Although both girls were active in the sand work process, they had difficulty making decisions and they appeared to be afraid to develop strategies for solving problems. Somehow they seemed to have overcompensated for their anger and now, in attempting to control their anger, they were unable to release any emotion. They had become extremely passive and reluctant to make decisions. This behavior could be observed in their sand tray work. For example, that day the two girls had taken turns yelling, "Green Monster, come and get me!" and each girl in turn had picked up Green Monster and moved it back and forth. The girl figure with the umbrella had called out and Green Monster moved toward her, and then the woman figure had called out and moved as if waving her blanket. This activity had continued for about 10 minutes. Julia had just sat in the corner, but Ms. Sandler thought she had noticed a slight movement of her head from side to side.

For the next session Bettina and Jollie showed up first. Julia arrived 5 minutes later and took her seat in the same corner, but this time she watched the activity in the sand tray. Bettina and Jollie again placed Green Monster in the center of the sand tray and repeated their previous activity. Julia sat and watched the activity in the sand tray. After a brief period she began shaking her head from side to side, and she suddenly arose from her seat. She yelled, "This is stupid! I can't watch these two doing this stupid stuff. I'm out of here."

Ms. Sandler asked, "Julia, do you think you can help them? Maybe you can do something else."

Julia, who by this time had reached the door, turned around and walked to the shelf, where she put her hand on the fire-breathing dragon. Bettina and Jollie stopped their seemingly interminable ritual and looked at Julia who said, "Keep going. Keep doing that distracting stupid stuff and I'll sneak up on Green Monster."

Bettina and Jollie restarted their ritual while the fire-breathing dragon entered the sand tray in back of Green Monster. Julia shouted, "Fire-Breathing Dragon pounces on Green Monster and burns him to a crisp!" Then she turned and said, "Now I'm really out of here."

Later that day, Ms. Sandler looked at the photograph of the sand tray left by the three girls. Green Monster was flat in the sand with Fire-Breathing Dragon on top. The girl with the umbrella and the woman with the blanket stood on the two sides of Green Monster but were closer to the monster than they had previously been.

After several sessions the three girls were actually forming a cooperative group. Julia had long traded the lamb for Fire-Breathing Dragon and most often solved situations by leaving a villainous monster in ashes. In the meantime, Bettina and Jollie were beginning to make decisions, and their figures demonstrated this. For example, Bettina suggested that they build a castle, and Jollie said that they could try to find a magic lamp that the bad king had stolen from their village. Julia agreed. Bettina and Jollie chose to keep the same figures, the girl with the umbrella and the woman with the blanket. Julia shook her head and said, "We'll need more than an umbrella and a blanket if we're going to attack a castle." Julia chose a new figure: a wizard with a tall hat and a big magic wand. The three girls cooperated in building a model of a castle with blocks and sand. Then the girls searched the shelves. First they found a miniature kettle and decided that it would be the magic lamp; they placed it in their castle. Jollie found a figure of a knight and Bettina found a figure of a king and placed them both at the top of their castle.

Bettina said, "They're at the top of the castle tower and that's a bad king."

Julia said, "I'm glad you two have an umbrella and a blanket to protect us from the evil king and all his knights." Jollie and Bettina ignored Julia's comment.

Again, at the end of the session, Ms. Sandler looked at the picture of their sand tray and smiled. The king and the knight were upside down with their heads deep in the sand. The three figures stood in a circle with the magic lamp in the middle. The story had started with Julia's wizard making a frontal assault on the castle. The wizard had used the magic wand to try to cast a spell over the king, but it hadn't worked; the king had more powerful magic, which was decided by a vote of 2 to 1. Meanwhile, the girl with the umbrella and the woman with the blanket climbed up the back of the castle and knocked the king and the knights off the top of the castle. Unfortunately, the king and knight landed on the wizard. The two at the top of the castle heard a whole army of knights running up the winding stairs to the tower. Umbrella Girl grabbed the magic lamp, opened her umbrella, and glided off the tower. Blanket Woman held her blanket up and caught a breeze and also glided down. The king had powerful magic; they had both survived the fall and were about to kill Wizard, but Blanket Woman and Umbrella Girl landed on them, and the king and the knight wound up with their heads in the sand. Apparently the king's magic didn't work when he was upside down with his head in the sand.

This sand tray activity initiated several similar stories in which Blanket Woman and Umbrella Girl rescued Julia's figure, which she regularly changed. As the weeks passed and the stories evolved, Julia's figure was repeatedly helped and rescued. Julia herself began to trust the other two girls. She demonstrated this by suggesting a story in which they were all sisters living with their mother, who was always drunk. They built rooms with blocks and furniture. Julia chose the figure of a woman reclining to represent the mother. Mother's major role was totally inconsistent with the erratic behaviors that serve as the hallmark for the Disconnection and Rejection core issue domain. In their sand tray activity, the girls developed strategies such as consoling one another after an abusive interaction with Mother. Julia began to develop trust in the girls, and it was evident that the three were quickly becoming friends. Her anger diminished, and the outbursts and sarcastic remarks subsided. Ms. Sandler opened her computer file with photos of this group's sand trays. The one of their final sand tray had Mother reclining on a couch while Umbrella Girl, Blanket Woman, and Lamb Butterfly sat together in a circle optimistically discussing their futures.

Summary

The two cases presented in this chapter demonstrate the use and effectiveness of sand tray work for addressing core issues in two very different circumstances. Kazzie had experienced a singular event: She had witnessed the deliberate killing of her dog. The sand tray work in her case seemed to provide her with the opportunity to represent her anger and her sadness. Although the pain of losing her dog would certainly remain, the immediate emotions subsided. In contrast, Julia's core issues involved her very toxic home situation. She was able to develop emotion-focused coping mechanisms to deal with a home environment that fell short of meeting her core emotional needs (Everly & Lating, 2004). A parent struggling with addiction is likely to be neither consistent nor fair, and as a result attachment to and trust in others quickly diminishes. Julia's physical safety was at risk, and there was a clear lack of emotional connection and order in her life. The experience of living with an alcoholic parent can have long-term negative effects. However, Julia was able to repair some of these core needs to connect with Bettina and Jollie. The three girls seemed to benefit very much from constructing a variety of worlds in sand trays.

Session after session each child would enter Ms. Sandler's office and see the smooth sand that had been made ready. Ms. Sandler knew it was critical that each session begin with clean and smooth sand. She documented her work with clients using a digital camera. In her notes, she remarked on how clients approached the sand tray, the worlds they created, their behavior, their energy, and the miniatures and figures they chose and placed in the tray. She also noted patterns that emerged during the session as well as those that repeated from session to session. She found it helpful to diagram action, energy, and patterns in the sand tray as well as the movement of objects during the session. Ms. Sandler commented on core issue themes that emerged, her conversations with her clients, and their progress over time. Ms. Sandler speculated in her notes about her clients' progress and set goals for the next time they met. She realized that these goals and plans could shift with client input and actions.

Sand work is a very effective technique to use with children, especially those 9 through 13 years of age. During this developmental stage in particular, children readily use symbols to represent their worlds. The sand appeals to children's need for energy and tactility and acts as a container for the anxiety and pain that many children in counseling face. The sand tray is a therapeutic tool that allows children the time and place to explore, create, and show counselors what they are experiencing. When children show their world, counselors can examine it with them, be present, and see how, week after week, these worlds change, evolve, and heal. This can be done with no words at all or with fewer words than are needed for traditional adult counseling interventions. We respect the sand tray, for there is much power in what can be communicated in sand.

creative artwork
in child counseling

This chapter provides an overview of how creative art can be used to help children who have difficulty expressing themselves or who struggle more than others with developing adequate coping skills and strategies. A case study is used to illustrate a counseling process that uses a creative art intervention to address the child's identified core issue.

The Case of Cameron

Ten-year-old Cameron softly stroked the canvas with his left hand. White paint dripped from the fingertips of his right hand and streaked the dark and heavy blackness he had spread across the canvas. Mr. Talent stood behind Cameron and gazed at the artwork unfolding before his eyes. A huge graveyard filled with white headstones and gray streaks of rain emerged. Mr. Talent strained to monitor a strong reaction. There was so much death in this child's world. He swelled with sadness, finding it hard to catch his breath, but as he glanced toward Cameron he noticed this young boy painted on, not looking the least bit stressed or grief stricken. The painting and the painter did not fit together; there was incongruence. Cameron looked at peace, and yet his art, a dreary sight, suggested a very different mood. The peaceful eeriness suggested a disconnection that puzzled Mr. Talent.

Designing Interventions That Tap Children's Creative Nature

One of the most endearing aspects of children is their unbridled desire to engage the world in a creative manner. Whether there are tools around or not, children will inevitably engage in acts of creativity. Children learn about their world and their roles in it by creating, rehearsing, and learning—by practicing life. That is their job, and they do it well. If children are handed something or find something, they usually will do something with it. What they do depends on their developmental stage.

Using artwork and creative interventions within counseling contexts produces therapeutic benefits (Wadeson, 1980). This is particularly true for younger clients. Art naturally holds the attention of most children (H. Gardner, 1980; Hagood, 2002; Kramer, 1979; Landreth, 2002a; Malchiodi, 1999; Oaklander, 1988; J. Rubin, 1984). Art provides an opportunity for the expression of emotions, thoughts, and ideas that may not be accessible through a verbal exchange (Chapman, Morabito, Ladakakos, Schrier, & Knudson, 2001; Malchiodi, 2008). Artwork unleashes creativity and produces something that provokes discussion and reflection. Intentionally or not, the very use of art materials produces a product (Malchiodi, 2006). The product promotes safety and defuses intensity; children can talk about "the product" and not themselves. This externalization provides a buffer from the intensity of a more direct and often more threatening discussion (DiLeo, 1983; Kramer & Schehr, 1983). Artwork itself is totally engrossing and yet it allows children to focus on the process of their creation. This can enhance emotional release and deflect pain (H. Gardner, 1980). Children can relax and often reenergize. Through the use of art in counseling, clients can try new things; they can dabble and experience creative ways to solve problems. The act of creating is an empowering activity from which new energy emerges. Through this form of expression, clients can experience themselves anew (Hagood, 2002; Landreth, 2002a; Oaklander, 1988). This can enhance the sense of self, resulting in a more integrated self; art promotes the mind–body connection (Malchiodi, 2003, 2005).

Working with creative materials within counseling contexts provides tools and strategies that are congruent with the developmental stage and cultural worldview of children and adolescents (Crenshaw, 2004, 2006; Malchiodi, 1999). It is through the creative process that young clients come to understand the world around them and learn how to better cope with—and in some cases master—their fears and anxieties (H. Gardner, 1980; Kramer & Schehr, 1983). Artwork provides an alternative means for children to express their personal narratives. Children learn by doing, not by sitting and talking (Landreth, 2002a). Children thrive in environments that offer multisensory opportunities: visual, tactile, auditory, kinesthetic, and even olfactory. Using art in counseling is a natural fit for most children (Oaklander, 1988).

The object created can prompt dialogue after the process is complete (Hagood, 2002; Malchiodi, 2008; Wadeson, 1980). In contrast to other therapeutic interventions, such as talk or even play therapy, art therapy provides a unique opportunity for the counselor to enter into a discussion about the full expression of what the child needs to communicate (Crenshaw, 2004; Oaklander, 1988). The time spent by the youngster in creating can prepare him or her for a safe discussion that can assist in developing insight (Malchiodi, 2005, 2006).

Underpinnings of Artwork With Children

Teachers have long understood the value of artwork in helping children to understand life situations, to express feelings, and to move through developmental stages (H. Gardner, 1980; Kramer, 1979; J. Rubin, 1984). Professionals in many fields have recognized the value of artwork as therapy. For example, medical practitioners have applied the use of art and recreational approaches to assist patients in healing, to distract them from severely debilitating medical conditions, and to help them adjust to disease and surgical interventions (Chapman et al., 2001; Hagood, 2002; Malchiodi, 1999). Within the world of art itself, two strands have emerged: those artists who support the notion of informed and enlightened art and those who emphasize the benefits of art to psychological processes (Kramer, 1979; Wadeson, 1980). Some therapists use art as their primary tool (Malchiodi, 2003). Indeed, as art therapy emerged as a form of psychotherapy it drew from disciplines such as education, psychology, medicine (J. Rubin, 1984), and, of course, the arts.

Art as a form of therapy has often been used to help children deal with serious psychological and emotional problems, such as family dissolution (Crenshaw, 2004), trauma (Hagood, 2002), health crises and poverty (Chapman et al., 2001; Malchiodi, 2008), and war and turmoil (Landreth, 2002a; Oaklander, 1988). As a prisoner in Terezin, a Nazi concentration camp, Friedl Dicker-Brandeis helped many children cope with their incarceration by teaching them to draw. As she was being deported from her home in Vienna, Austria, she could only choose to bring a very limited number of possessions. Because she was an artist, she deliberately packed mostly art supplies. Friedl knew that art would be important for herself, and as it turned out, her ability to construct and to teach art helped hundreds of children cope with the horrors they were enduring. She knew that through artwork, the children could be comforted. Her art created some sense of beauty and optimism and helped the children cope and develop a sense of hope (S. G. Rubin, 2000). Prisoners in a Nazi concentration camp were not likely to cope successfully using problem-focused strategies. It also seems obvious that the core emotional needs of these children were being greatly inhibited (Young, 1990, 1999; Young et al., 2003). The children were in danger of rapidly losing secure attachments, leading to disconnection and rejection. They were likely suffering from impaired autonomy and performance with severely restricted limits and with few opportunities for spontaneity and play. Friedl was able to use the creative arts to help these children cope. Living with constant threats and frequent demands would have taxed or exceeded the resources of any child. By using art to enhance positive emotion-focused coping, Friedl was using art therapeutically.

Today, universities and art therapist training programs offer specific coursework in how to become an art therapist. However, many professional counselors include art within the context of a wider repertoire of counseling techniques for children, and they find that art has many therapeutic benefits (Chapman et al., 2001; Crenshaw, 2006; Hagood, 2002).

The Counselor Who Uses Art

Mr. Talent, a former teacher turned professional school counselor, used art as one of many techniques within his child counseling practice. When Mr. Talent endeavored to set up his counseling practice at the Snake River Wellness Center, he wanted to create a workroom that was inviting. And he succeeded. Metaphorically speaking, his clinical environment spoke volumes. Children and parents would walk into the office, and the message was clear: "In here it is okay to get messy," or "In here you can relax," or "In here you are carefree." Mr. Talent wanted his tools (his art materials) to help the thoughts and feelings of his children to come alive. Art was his preferred technique for getting them to externalize their emotions. Mr. Talent wanted to assist children and engage them in their stories. He had great respect for their work and creativity. He hypothesized that art was an extension of the child's self. He also realized that the process of art making produced a visual record. Not only was it rewarding, but it created opportunities for problem solving. Usually he would use a child's drawing as a way to initiate a discussion, but only after the child had completed the work. He realized that discussing a work in progress could interfere with the therapeutic benefits and alter the product as it was being created.

Mr. Talent reflected on his recent session with Cameron. He had not had enough time to explore Cameron's drawing of the graves and, given the very brief amount of time left in that session, he had thought it inadvisable to initiate a discussion that would have had to be ended too abruptly. Mr. Talent lifted Cameron's latest picture from the storage drawer. He scanned it carefully, trying to find some answers and some hidden meanings. He mused, "What was there in this work of Cameron's that he could not see that captured the narrative?" He decided to talk with Cameron about his art during their next session that afternoon.

Later that same day Cameron stood and looked at his drawing, a picture with a similar landscape of white headstones. Cameron smiled and seemed to be quite satisfied with his painting. Mr. Talent paused. He stated with encouragement, "Cameron, tell me about this picture."

Cameron looked up at Mr. Talent and said, "This is my PopPop."

There were no people in the painting, but Mr. Talent was hopeful that this might be a major breakthrough. He wanted to ask "Are you in there?" or "Is your grandfather buried somewhere in there?" But he did not ask those questions. Calmly, he said, "Tell me more."

Cameron's grandmother explained that they were both dealing with the recent death of her husband, Cameron's grandfather. Although they were sad, she felt that she had made her peace. However, Cameron continued struggling with the death of his beloved PopPop. He did not understand why PopPop had gone away. He would cover his ears when his grandmother explained that his PopPop had died. He demonstrated his deep denial by shouting, "No! No! He's not dead! He can't be dead!"

Cameron had lived with his grandmother and PopPop since birth after the death of both of his parents. PopPop had been a Native American,

Shoshone, and both he and his wife, Cameron's grandmother, were devout Catholics. They drew from a varied support system and rich religious beliefs. They especially drew from rich cultural traditions regarding death and PopPop's transcending into another world. The family lived near but not on the Shoshone Bannock reservation in southeastern Idaho. Mr. Talent had studied the Shoshone culture and asked Cameron's grandmother many questions. She was a practicing Roman Catholic, so he discussed culture and religious beliefs, especially as they related to matters of death. According to his grandmother, Cameron had never been a talkative little boy. Cameron and his grandfather had spent a great deal of time together. She said, "Those two were always busy doing a lot of things, but they would say almost nothing. PopPop would work at something and Cameron would watch and then without a word Cameron would pick something up and do exactly what his PopPop had done." Since his grandfather's death, Cameron had become more withdrawn. He wanted to quit the Boy Scouts and was not doing well in school. He spent most of his time in his room, apparently doing nothing.

Processing the Artwork

Mr. Talent had many questions that he wanted answered. Nevertheless, patiently and true to how he had been trained, he let Cameron tell his story of what the art and the graveyard scene meant. Mr. Talent considered several things before he approached Cameron and processed his artwork. Mr. Talent had a background in art. He had been an art teacher and had earned a dual undergraduate degree in fine art and education before becoming a professional counselor. He therefore had a background in the use of art techniques and materials. His work area was well organized and filled with materials appropriate for the developmental stages of his clients. Counselors who use art usually acquire their materials after they have established their practice, but Mr. Talent had come prepared. As part of his counselor education program, Mr. Talent had also prepared by dealing with some control and personal issues. He felt no need to control the session and readily surrendered the session to the client. His clients took charge of their sessions while he provided a framework, guidelines, and support. He practiced client-initiated counseling. He embraced opportunities for his clients to have new experiences. He gained informed consent from parents and clients (Landreth, 2002a). A release of information was also obtained to ensure that their work could be photographed and saved for supervision and for future reference (Malchiodi, 2006).

Mr. Talent thought back on his first session with Cameron. The boy had walked into the workroom, looked around wide eyed, and exclaimed, "There sure is a lot of art stuff in here! This looks like a classroom."

Mr. Talent responded, "No, this is not a classroom, because in here kids get to do art without any pressure of grades. I have many art tools for children to work out their worries."

Cameron responded, "I suck at art," to which Mr. Talent said, "Well, in here you get to do art and it doesn't matter if you are a good artist or not. That's not important. So you get to try a lot of stuff without having to be perfect." Cameron nodded agreeably.

Reassuring a child and relaxing "art fears" is critical to any work with a client, and Cameron's relaxed posture indicated he was reassured (Malchiodi, 1999). Mr. Talent used both structured and unstructured techniques with his children depending on their presenting concerns, individual needs, and time constraints (Hagood, 2002). To Cameron he said, "Today we are going to work together using art. Why don't you create something that you are thinking about or maybe something that has given you worries?"

Mr. Talent recalled that Cameron stood for a few minutes looking around the room, taking in all the tools and supplies on the shelves. Then he put on an artist's apron and walked over to the easel. Cameron picked up a brush, dipped it into a jar, and smeared the chart paper with black paint. He said not a word. He painted. His body was fully engaged, as his muscles from head to toe moved with each stroke of the brush. Mr. Talent knew not to reflect at that time. He knew not to break Cameron's concentration (Crenshaw, 2004, 2006). He did not want to risk leading his client during the art process. However, he paid very careful attention to Cameron's use of media, his hesitations, his rhythm, what he painted, and the energy shifts and changes (Wadeson, 1980). He observed changes that Cameron made, especially when he wiped off part of the painting with a rag.

As Cameron slowly walked back from the table, he glanced at the painting, smiled, and said, "I am finished. Can I go now?"

Mr. Talent looked at the clock, bit his lip, and hesitated. There was little time for a lengthy discussion, little time to uncover what was hidden in that drawing or what was buried in that graveyard. Something powerful was represented in that painting. The ambiguity of the graves and the smile stirred Mr. Talent to suggest one additional attempt to solve the mystery.

Counselors who use art as part of their therapeutic process understand that clients need to process their experience (Kramer & Schehr, 1983). However, children cannot or do not always talk about their products (H. Gardner, 1980; Landreth, 2002a; Malchiodi, 1999). So that day, Mr. Talent said, "Yes, you could leave now but we have three more minutes to work today. You get to decide how to spend the last three minutes."

Cameron said, "May I play with Mr. Siggy?"

"Oh certainly," was the reply.

And in the last 3 minutes, Cameron picked up the pet guinea pig and stroked him and sang him a lullaby. His shoulders hung relaxed as he snuggled Mr. Siggy. After 3 minutes, Cameron gently returned Mr. Siggy to his cage. Then he rose and calmly exited the room.

Mr. Talent thought and thought about Cameron's pictures . . . so many white headstones, seems like so much death. The last-minute attempt to solve the mystery had not worked as Mr. Talent had hoped.

After those two sessions Mr. Talent called Cameron's grandmother. She said that Cameron was improving. He was more engaged with school again and had started going back to scouting meetings. The day of the phone call Cameron had asked her to take him to the cemetery, something they had not done since PopPop had been buried.

During their third session Cameron returned to his painting of the graveyard. Mr. Talent quietly watched him work for several minutes. Then Cameron turned and said, "It is almost done."

Mr. Talent responded, "Sounds like you have just a little more to do."

Cameron nodded and proceeded. He added two small dots in the huge row of headstones. "Now I am done."

Mr. Talent said, "Tell me about this picture."

Again, Cameron said, "This is me and PopPop." He looked directly up at Mr. Talent as if to say, "Isn't it obvious?"

Mr. Talent, at a total loss, said, "Tell me more about you and PopPop."

Then Cameron explained, very patiently because Mr. Talent clearly was missing the big picture, "There we are." He pointed to the two small black dots. "PopPop and me are doing our rounds. He's there now all by himself."

Taking a thorough history is always important, but seasoned counselors know some pieces of information are always lacking. Sometimes not having this information can cause a counselor to misinterpret the symbols and meaning of a child's artwork. In Cameron's case, it would have been easy to assume that the cemetery and pictures of headstones represented a child in the throes of grief and loss, a child obsessed with death. But Cameron's paintings were more complex. His paintings of headstones represented not merely death but much more—his love for his grandfather. The paintings were his way of remembering the time they had spent together taking many loving walks through the veterans' cemetery where his grandfather had been a volunteer caretaker. Cameron's denial of his grandfather's death was a negative emotion-focused coping strategy. His artwork helped him move through that denial to the use of positive coping strategies involving acceptance. In so doing, he was able to emerge back into his world.

The Counseling Artwork Room

To use art as part of their repertoire, child counselors do not have to become registered art therapists. However, they do need some preparation and training in the use of art with clients (Kramer, 1979; Malchiodi, 2003, 2005, 2006; Wadeson, 1980). Artwork is powerful and elicits strong responses from clients. Medium matters, and counselors must have training in selecting the appropriate tools (J. Rubin, 1984).

Mr. Talent had carefully selected the materials for his counseling artwork room. He gazed about the room and considered the value of the many materials. He knew how to use them with his clients and what they could elicit during a counseling session. Furthermore, he understood the advantages and disadvantages of particular art media. Many baskets were easily retrievable and filled with a variety of art tools. One basket included various pencils, many black, gray, or charcoal but others with very bright colors. He also had very large erasers. He knew that the pencils provided clients with a sense of refined control and the permission to erase as desired. However, he also knew that pencils can remind clients of negative school experiences. Other baskets were filled with pictures and precut materials that could be used for collage work to inspire clients who felt less artistically inclined. Mr. Talent had a bucket filled with felt pens of all colors, shapes, and sizes. Clients were usually familiar with these tools and were more inclined to work with them; they involved a smooth motion and could easily cover over other lines that had been drawn. Felt pens provided some control, but because they were permanent, they were also risky. There was also a disadvantage because, when left uncapped, they quickly dried out. Mr. Talent looked up at the top shelf, where several wicker baskets were filled with oil-based crayons and chalk. These allowed for blending and blurring boundaries. Some clients chose these tools to express regression. Although for some clients oil crayons and chalk provided a welcome opportunity to get messy, for others these media provoked anxiety and concerns about getting "dirty." Mr. Talent had a large bowl filled with various oil-based sculpting clays. He had play dough for younger children because it was easier for their small hands to manipulate. Clay and dough were three-dimensional media of creation.

In sculpting work, clients create characters and posture them in a variety of actions. The impermanent nature of the clay can be frustrating to some clients, whereas other clients seem pleased that they can easily correct or change what they may consider to be mistakes. Mr. Talent's collection of paints included poster paint, watercolors, oils, and fingerpaints. Some of the paints were bold in color and prompted creativity and the expression of drama and strong feelings. Their goal was to free clients for deep emotional exploration or, for some, to be out of control and even to get dirty. In other baskets, there were low-heat glue guns and multidimensional objects such as beads, sticks, and creative crafts that clients could use as principal media or integrate with other media. If there was one disadvantage to his art room, it was that so many choices could overwhelm some clients. To mitigate this potential problem, Mr. Talent kept things organized and as uncluttered as possible. He had a work table, but there were also two comfortable chairs for clients who may have been more inclined to sit and talk rather than to do art.

Mr. Talent knew that interpreting art is a tricky business. He had read widely on the topic of Jungian archetypes and symbols, particularly as these relate to specific cultures and religious beliefs. He tended to shy away from books that made strong claims regarding what certain symbols and animals might mean. He paid more attention to the process and the production of the art and what he learned about his clients when they were creating and talking about their own work (Crenshaw, 2006; Malchiodi, 2006).

He understood that children used color in various ways depending on their developmental stage, creative drive, and emotional needs (DiLeo, 1983). Children instinctively know that the sun is yellow, clouds are blue or white, and a chimney is often brick red (H. Gardner, 1980). It is the unconventional use of color that prompts examination. Colors are also emotionally laden, but they do not always represent the same emotion (Malchiodi, 2005; Wadeson, 1980). For example, red may represent anger, but it may also represent blood or passion, love, happiness, a joyful spirit, a wedding, or a heart—sometimes loving, sometimes broken. The appropriate interpretation is more often found within the client than in a book. With this in mind, Mr. Talent tried to take his cues from his child clients and was often surprised how his preconceived impressions about meanings were cancelled out by a child's simple explanation. Analyses of children's artwork can result in misinterpretations that can endanger the therapeutic process. It is important to listen to the child explain the meaning of any creative work. Nothing is universal. To interpret in isolation does a disservice to a client (J. Rubin, 1984).

Summary

The use of creative artwork in counseling can help children who are otherwise unable to develop coping strategies. This was the case for the children in Terezin, a Nazi concentration camp, many of whom Friedl Dicker-Brandeis helped cope by teaching them to draw (S. G. Rubin, 2000). When situational conditions are such that the problem itself cannot be changed, then a young client will attempt to use emotion-focused coping strategies. These have the potential to be negative. However, counseling approaches, such as the use of creative artwork, can redirect coping to more positive strategies.

A child's core issues are not simple, and interpretations that provide simple answers can interfere in the counseling process. Mr. Talent did not jump to a single interpretation of Cameron's drawings. He understood that they were far more complex than they appeared at first glance. His nondirective approach to counseling helped him come to an understanding of Cameron's issues, while engaging in creative artwork helped Cameron release pent-up feelings about the death of his grandfather. His coping strategy evolved from painting graves to requesting to visit the cemetery. Art was the conduit for his acceptance of his grandfather's death. The process of creating artwork can help many people, especially children, work toward acquiring positive coping strategies.

consulting with parents and professional stakeholders

Many counselors who work with children argue that the most difficult part of their work is not assessment or clinical intervention but dealing with parents and the other professionals who are immersed in the lives of their child clients. The challenges counselors face when their role changes from clinician to consultant are noteworthy. Collaborating and consulting with parents and professional stakeholders demands a very different skill set from that needed to work solely with child clients. In this chapter we discuss the communication and consulting skills that facilitate successful relationships with parents, caregivers, and professionals.

Parents and frequently teachers are the most influential people in the lives of child clients. Parents and teachers spend far greater amounts of time with the children than counselors do. They are also privy to information and observations that counselors are not. Thus, counselors must consider themselves one player on a team consisting of individuals who care about the child, and the whole team must be focused on the same desired outcomes. Much can be gained from engaging in consultation relationships with parents and other professionals. According to Kottman (2003), consulting with parents and other professionals, particularly teachers, is critical to achieving successful counseling outcomes. It stands to reason, therefore, that counselors should work to become aware of some of the stumbling blocks in consultation. In this way, they will be better prepared to deal with the various situations that are likely to emerge in clinical practice.

The Challenges

Counselors face specific challenges in consulting with parents and professionals (Mullen, 2003). If one accepts the premise that moving from counselor to consultant and even at times advocate is in fact challenging, then it would be very useful to have a thematic framework for addressing the obstacles one is like to encounter.

Applying a Broad Developmental Knowledge Base

Many adults do not truly understand the nature of children and the complexities of their developmental stages. In our work, we have discovered that both parents and professionals—even some mental health and educational professionals—have a limited knowledge of child development. In fact, someone who is considering working with children but who does not have a very strong knowledge base regarding the clinical implications of development across the biological, cognitive, and affective domains should take immediate steps to acquire these understandings. Knowledge and competence promote ethical practice. Because so much happens during childhood to set various core issues in motion, counselors must be able to understand the function of development in this important aspect of assessment (Halstead, 2007).

Let us assume that the counselor indeed has a strong knowledge base and understanding of child development. Most parents do not. When counselors try to collaborate and consult with parents regarding the nature of their children's core issue struggles, the parents' lack of knowledge becomes a critical issue to which counselors must attend. To illustrate this, we can use a clinical example. A mother of a 5-year-old boy called the child counseling clinic wanting counseling services for her son. The intake counselor gathered the necessary demographics and asked the mother what her concerns were. The mother stated, "All he wants to do is play." With all due respect to the mother, our team just did not see that as a problem or concern that needed to be "fixed"—especially through play therapy interventions. Our understanding of child development tells us that it is perfectly normal for a 5-year-old to want to play all the time. In fact, we are delighted to hear concerns such as this in a clinical setting because most of the children with whom we work are dealing with some form of trauma that impedes their basic expression of what it is to be children. The problem in this case is how we as counselors demonstrate respect for the mother's perspective that there is something wrong with her boy while simultaneously providing her with information so that she may be more accepting of her son. Helping the mother gain additional knowledge as to what constitutes normal development and the important role of play for a 5-year-old will help to build a more supportive environment within the family.

It can be even more frustrating when a professional lacks sufficient knowledge of the developmental tasks of childhood. This can derail the counselor's attempts to collaborate and consult successfully. Although a life-span human development course is standard in most counseling programs, specific coursework addressing clinical assessment and counseling interventions that focus on children is not. Therefore, even though it is often assumed that all mental health professionals speak the same language, many have never taken coursework specific to developmental assessment in childhood or child-focused interventions (Mullen, 2003). A lack of specific education and experience in this area can make collaboration efforts and consultations stressful. Our clinical perspective is that work with children must always be filtered through the lens of development and that developmental factors serve as a basic foundation upon which successful interventions are built. Without this lens, other professionals might not be able to access a conceptual understanding of this working orientation.

Another example illustrates this point. Bill was a 7-year-old Euro-American boy who lived with his foster care parents and had regular visits with his biological parents and his 5-year-old biological sister, Emma, who lived in a separate foster care placement. The children had both been removed from the home because of neglect, domestic violence, and parental drug abuse. From this information alone the counselor would consider initial core issues hypotheses associated with the Disconnection and Rejection domain, such as mistrust/abuse, abandonment/instability, emotional deprivation, and so forth (Halstead, 2007). Important consideration must also be given to how the hypothesized core issues manifest within the emotional world of the child. Having engaged Bill in 12 sessions of child-centered counseling, the counselor attended a service provider's meeting for Bill. This meeting included Bill's counselor, his biological parents, his foster care parents, the Department of Social Services protective caseworker, the family social worker, and his sister's primary counselor. Bill's foster care parents stated that Bill was wetting the bed nightly and this action seemed purposeful. Bill had been wearing child-size pull-up diapers at night because bedwetting had been an ongoing problem. The foster parents had discovered that during the night Bill would actually pull down the protective diaper and urinate on his bed, on his dresser, and in his closet. This situation created a good deal of extra work each day in terms of laundry and cleaning. The foster parents reported that there was now a constant odor of urine in their home. They had tried many conventional ways of helping Bill with this problem, including limiting his fluid intake during the evening, having him void before bed, and waking him during the night to do so again. None of these interventions alleviated the problem.

The counselor proposed an idea based on her understanding of Bill's core issues (abuse/mistrust) and her assessment of his avoidance coping strategy (Halstead, 2007). She suggested that the foster parents place a bucket lined with a plastic bag in Bill's room so that he could urinate whenever he needed to do so. They all laughed at the suggestion. The counselor, using the core issues framework, explained to the group that during her sessions with Bill it was very clear that he was very focused on using different methods and strategies to avoid future abuse and had a difficult time believing that he was ever safe. Based on this framing of the problem it would make sense within Bill's emotional world that spraying urine could be a protective strategy. The group became attentive. The counselor went on to explain that for a very long period, Bill's bedroom at nighttime had not been a safe place. It was there that he would be awakened and abused. The fact that the counselor's explanation made intuitive sense won over the foster care parents, who agreed to try this new intervention for just 1 week. Bill responded favorably by using the pail and stopped wetting the bed, dresser, and closet. The knowledgeable counselor was able to translate Bill's behaviors to a group of well-meaning but uninformed adults in a manner that allowed them to better understand what motivated this child to engage in a set of troubling behaviors.

Using a core issues framework as a basis for understanding the problem and filtering it through the lens of a concrete operational reality helped make it clear to others that fear and an extreme need for safety were at play. When these two forces converged, Bill began to seek very concrete strategies to keep others away from him. The net result was his antisocial behavior. The counselor honored Bill's core issue reality and was able to do so in a manner that was consistent with his developmental stage. The difficulty in providing effective consultation is that others often do not have a strong understanding of the complexities of core issue problems and how they may be expressed differently across different developmental stages. As this example illustrates, counselors can gain a reasonable amount of credibility by using the core issues framework to explain the nature of the underlying problem and how it manifests in the child's relational world (Halstead, 2007).

Explaining the Nature of Counseling Interventions and Anticipated Outcomes

Another challenge related to consulting involves helping others understand the nature of the interventions that will be implemented or the outcomes one can reasonably expect as a result of counseling sessions. When adults seek out counseling services for children, they usually do so in response to a prolonged period of stress. Often adults are frustrated because they have tried every possible intervention they can think of and have failed to alleviate the problem. Thus it is understandable that the parent or guardian would want to know what the counselor is going to do that has not already been tried and when he or she could likely expect some sort of positive outcome. Anyone who has been in this situation knows that at times counselors struggle to explain how counseling "works." This is made all the more challenging when they must try to explain the nature of play, narrative, sand tray, and art as therapies while relating those modalities to developmentally sound interventions. This is especially true when the audience understands counseling through a narrow lens that includes only "talking" interventions. Establishing credibility and legitimacy with parents is critical. Having a well thought out and succinct explanation of how one works with children and how counseling is designed to create desired outcomes will go far to boost the counselor's credibility. One can produce information sheets or short booklets that provide foundational material that sensitizes and educates the parent. This material can be sent to the home in advance so that more of the actual consultation period can be spent answering additional questions that emerge. Providing this written material can help ensure that the parent has been well informed prior to the start of the counselor working with the child.

The same strategy can be used with members of the professional mental health and educational communities. Preparing written materials specifically for other professionals can help establish some common ground for the helping services that overlap while informing other service providers about the unique nature of the counselor's role.

Managing Relational Boundaries

Another challenge is negotiating the complex dynamic of maintaining respect for the counselor–child relationship while simultaneously providing useful information during consultation (Mullen, 2003). For work with minors, the parameters of confidentiality are broader than those for work with adults. When consent forms and releases are signed, a counselor can share information with parents, other care providers, as well as service providers, including teachers. Authorizations of this nature should be specific to what other service providers would need to know to provide the best services to the child. Because they are minors, children have little say in what information is shared and with whom. The therapist must find ways of sharing relevant information without jeopardizing the confidentiality of a session. Communicating too much information can put a carefully built therapeutic relationship at risk. The counselor must instead decide how much information needs to be disclosed so that the appropriate services can be recommended and accessed. To do this, the counselor must be sensitive to the child's developmental stage. He or she needs to attend to how much the child has developed a sense of a private world and needs to become increasingly judicious about sharing information as the child grows and matures.

When the challenge of what to share with parents and professionals arises in the consulting relationship, we suggest only sharing specifics when necessary. During a sandplay session, June, an 11-year-old, created an elaborate sand tray. June's therapy focused around her history of having been sexually molested by Jerry, a 17-year-old neighbor. The sand tray June created had rigid boundaries and several characters. Two characters, one of whom she called a "demon" and the other a "good guy," were placed strategically around the figurine of a young girl. Upon finishing her creation she pointed to the two figures and began to cry. She said to Lindee, her counselor, "These two are both Jerry. He was really nice sometimes but then he hurt me too." She shared with the counselor that she liked some of the special attention but hated "what he did to me and how it felt." When June came out of the session, the rims of her eyes were still red. Lindee told June's mother Ms. DeMey, "June worked very hard during our session today." Ms. DeMey asked if she could call Lindee to discuss some new concerns she had, and Lindee encouraged her to do so.

When Ms. DeMey called Lindee, she started out by stating that she really did have some new concerns, but she also really wanted to know what had happened in the session because June had gone right to bed when they had returned home even though it was only 6 p.m. Lindee did not share the details of the sand creation or discuss what June had shared with her with regard to her feelings about Jerry. She instead said, "Ms. DeMey, I know that you care for June so much. She feels so supported by you. You never push her with regard to the details of her session. June knows her counseling sessions are a safe place for her to share her feelings. Today's session was difficult because June is working hard to make sense of what happened to her. This is still hard for her to understand. You have done so much to encourage her, especially since she disclosed the molestation." Ms. DeMey shared how guilty she felt that she had not protected her daughter and how she still felt helpless, which was why she kept pressing for specifics; she wanted to make sense of it all. It is here, in such a moment, when the counselor's skills as a listener can build an alliance with the parent to create for the child a higher quality support system. Lindee honored Ms. DeMey but at the same time demonstrated a shared respect for June.

An alternative way of sharing the details of work done with a child is to focus on core issue themes and improvements that emerge as the work progresses. These observations are often glossed over by professionals and parents, who are focused on pathology and the end gain. When individuals are focused only on the ultimate desired outcomes, there can be a tendency to rush the counseling process. In these cases, it is useful to talk with a parent about meaningful stages in his or her child's progress that can be recognized and applauded as important steps toward an end point (Mullen, 2007).

Establishing a Clear Professional Specialization

Counselors who work with children, especially those whose professional identity might be aligned with sandplay therapy, play therapy, or another creative counseling milieu, should define their scope of practice, earn appropriate credentials, and display these credentials. These credentials can be highlighted in clinical materials and brochures, on business cards, and in selected advertisements. Bolstering expertise with additional certifications, trainings, and clinical supervision enhances a practitioner's credibility for consulting or collaborating with parents, teachers, and medical and mental health professionals. Counselors should work toward creating a strong professional affiliation with organizations that assess and support continued professional development within their specialization (e.g., play, sand tray, narrative, or art therapy). Competent professionals develop a strong professional identification and align themselves with relevant professional associations and organizations. Supervision and peer review are critical to continued growth, learning, and professional support and help counselors avoid the pitfalls of clinical isolation. When counselors feel more competent and confident about their work, they are able to demonstrate this in the context of consultation and collaboration.

Guiding Principles for Practice

When opportunities for collaboration and consultation arise, counselors should do whatever they can to make the process a positive experience for parents and professionals alike. Those who find value in the counseling process are much more likely to apply elements of the information and help that is offered. Applying some basic principles will go a long way toward helping counselors be more effective.

Axline (1947) developed eight core principles for counselors who practice child-centered play interventions. Although she addressed play therapists specifically, her principles apply to all counseling work involving children, their parents, and other professionals. She cautioned that although her principles sounded simple, using each to produce a desired outcome could prove to be very challenging. What follows is our adaptation of Axline's original principles for play therapy to respectful collaboration and consultation with parents and professionals. Although these guidelines link directly to Axline's principles, we have adapted and extended them to apply to all forms of counseling interventions with children. Finally, it is important to note that each one of these principles flows directly from and directly into the others, so one would benefit from thinking of all eight principles as a package.

Principle 1:
Form a Strong Working Relationship With Parents, Caretakers, and Professionals

Like Axline, we suggest an approach to consultation and collaboration that focuses on building a strong alliance with the parent, caretaker, or professional with whom the child also has contact. This relationship forms the foundation for quality collaboration and consultation efforts. Child counselors must work to develop this working relationship as quickly as possible. Once counselors have built rapport, they stand a much better chance of adding to the knowledge base of parents and professionals as long as they do so by gently offering additional or clarifying information.

Principle 2:
Accept Parents, Caretakers, and Other Helping Professionals and Their Ideas

It has been suggested that a successful consultation process results from engaging others in an appreciative, nonjudgmental atmosphere in which positive and specific strategies for monitoring child behavior are considered and there is a focus on improving child–parent communication (Sommers-Flanagan, 2007). This view supports not only accessing information from others but also providing opportunities for others to expand the conversation based on a core issues assessment. Consider Chuck, who shows many signs of struggling with a core issue of vulnerability to harm or illness:

Professional: I am Chuck's classroom teacher and I spend a lot of time with him.

Counselor: You know so much about Chuck. I am really hoping that you can serve as an important resource to help me fill in some missing information. I have been struck by Chuck's sense of fear and dread. He seems so vulnerable at times. Have you ever been aware of this in your classroom? If so, do you have any ideas as to what helps when he works himself into this fearful state?

Counselors communicate to the child's parents that the latter are the experts on their own children. Sommers-Flanagan (2007) evaluated the use of a consultation model in which the consultant refrained from making negative or critical comments about parenting practices to the parent and focused on communicating empathy. Parents in the study did not make a single negative comment about the consultant. We suggest that counselors let parents know that what the parents think is going on with their children is important. Ask them about what they have tried, what has worked, and what has not. Giving parents the chance to provide information to aid the process in and of itself forms a bond and makes a clear statement of respect and dignity. This one-on-one consultation seems to carry much more weight with parents than a parenting class or support group. These approaches are consistent with other current trends in counseling that support this type of interaction (De Jong & Berg, 2002; Sommers-Flanagan & Sommers-Flanagan, 2004).

Principle 3:
Establish a Feeling of Safety So That Feelings Can Be Expressed

This principle is very closely related to building a strong working relationship described in Principle 1. However, it emphasizes the importance of establishing a feeling of safety in which the other person can share his or her perspective.

Communicating with children is qualitatively different than communicating with adults, yet many adults have a difficult time really grasping the implications of this. Consultation and collaboration allow counselors to explain this phenomenon. It is difficult for some parents and professionals to understand how healing, change, and growth can happen if the "problem" is not addressed verbally. Most adults just have to be helped to understand that children are uniquely different from adults and thus a whole different means of communication must be used. Because this is a very common problem, it comes up repeatedly in parent caretaker consultation sessions. Nevertheless, the counselor needs to exercise caution when an adult does not understand some aspect of a child's world. Providing a safe environment in which the parent can see the child through an alternative lens is paramount. Counselors should never engage in language or tone that might be perceived as smug or condescending.

We have found that when confronted with this type of situation, it is often effective to tell a short story that illustrates the element that we want the parent to learn. This kind of "teaching story" provides a clear message that learning can take place at any point in one's parenting career. The following story told to a parent by a counselor illustrates this technique:

> It was never clear to me just how much I have to work sometimes to really understand young children. In fact, just the other day I was in the car with one of my own kids. Andrew, who is five, was trying to tell the rest of the family something. He was taking what seemed like forever to express what he wanted us to know. Finally, frustrated, I said to him, "Andrew, you have to tell us what you want now or else we won't be able to give you what you need." He stopped and said nothing. Then a few minutes later he came out with a message that stopped me right in my tracks. He said, "Sometimes my mouth and brain are not lined up and I cannot get the words out."

This story exemplifies how the counselor can discuss difficult topics, such as the fact that no one knows exactly how to parent perfectly all the time, and sometimes we all fall short. At the same time, it is possible to improve our parenting. We can always learn more about what our children need from us, and we need to be aware when these realizations occur. According to Sommers-Flanagan (2007), counselors must support parents with a sense of reassurance that they are on this journey together and that there is always another chance to do better.

Principle 4:
Recognize the Feelings Expressed During Consultation

Just as accessing affect is a crucial aspect of the counseling process, it is also important to foster the expression of feelings in consultation. Of course, forming a strong relationship and establishing a safe environment are key. The goal is to hear the feelings that are being expressed and to directly or indirectly reflect those feelings back to the parent or professional. Attending to affect in a supportive manner can not only result in greater insight but also increase the likelihood that such sharing continues in future sessions. Following are two examples from recent consultation sessions:

Situation 1

Professional: I am not in favor of play therapy services.
Counselor: So you are apprehensive about what play therapy can do to help this child's situation. Tell me more about this concern.

Situation 2

Professional: I don't see how playing will get this child to speak in school.
Counselor: You're worried because play therapy doesn't directly address the issue. I can see why that would be a concern. You really are a strong advocate for this child. Let me tell what I am noticing . . .

It is important to remember that the feelings adults express are informed by their perceptions. Grave concerns about a child's well-being can be eased, in many cases, by focusing attention on gains that are being made as opposed to the fact that end goals have not been reached. For example, the counselor might point out that the child who refused to speak at school or with adults outside the home is now using puppets to whisper directions to the counselor during counseling sessions. Although that same child is still not speaking to most adults in or outside of school, she has indeed made a change in a positive and prosocial direction. Often such information can ease the anxiety of caring adults.

Principle 5:
Respect Others' Abilities to Solve Their Own Problems

Sometimes when a parent is struggling with a very complex decision about his or her child's situation, it can be very difficult to trust the process. However, trusting in that process is an extremely important aspect of the counselor's role in consultation. As a consultant, the counselor must never extend beyond providing information, clarification, and support. The responsibility for making choices about the child (so long as they do not endanger the child) and instituting change in the home really belongs to the parent. Although there is clearly some shared responsibility among stakeholders, the counselor cannot assume responsibility that rightfully belongs to others in the child's life. Rather, he or she must support the parents in coming to their own conclusions and believe that when given enough information, opportunity, and responsibility, parents will make an adequate decision.

Parent: I don't know what to do. What should I do?
Counselor: You feel pressured to decide right now, and you are not really sure which way to go at this point.
Parent: Yes. Just tell me. Pick something for me to do and I will do it.
Counselor: I know this is a tough place for you to be in right now, and it must be all the harder that I am sitting here and not telling you what you should do.
Parent: Yes. That is it exactly. Can't you just tell me?
Counselor: Becky, I respect your ability to make a wise and thoughtful decision about your own child. The truth is I cannot just tell you what to do. This is a decision that you must make. We have sorted through your alternatives and the pros and cons attached to each one. I know that because you love Katie you will do what is best. I do want you to know, however, that I am ready to stand by you and by the decision you ultimately reach.

Principle 6:
Provide Space for Parents, Caretakers, and Professionals to Share Their Knowledge

As the consultation process unfolds, it will become increasingly clear that parents and professionals alike will work toward exercising their expertise regarding the child client. Counselors should be prepared for this dynamic to emerge. They accept this personal form of knowing. They understand how the other has come to gain this knowledge and the various ways in which it applies to particular children. This allows the other adults to lead and address their own agendas first. It also allows counselors to assess the depth of others' knowledge bases and point out any obstacles that might be present.

One downside of any form of personal knowing, of course, is that it can involve faulty logic. This best strategy we have found for dealing with poorly informed "truths" is responding with curiosity and asking for additional information. For example, if a parent or care provider offers information that directly contradicts normal child development, it is not in the counselor's best interest to directly confront the error. Rather, we suggest that the counselor state, "Wow, I've never heard that before," or "I can see why you might be concerned; let me look up some information for you," and then approach the topic with the caregivers again at a later date with data that educate. We have found it effective to provide easy-to-read literature no more than a page in length and to hint that it will reinforce much of what the parent might already know. Over time the counselor can develop fact sheets that address a variety of issues and use these again and again in practice. This approach creates a sense of acceptance and allows parents to let down their defenses so that they can be open to considering alternative perspectives regarding their child.

Principle 7:
Set Time Aside for Parents, Caretakers, and Professionals So That Conversations Are Not Rushed or Pressured

Counselors and children are well served by providing ample opportunity for adult stakeholders to be heard. This cannot be done by engaging in a brief exchange when the parent arrives prior to or at the end of a counseling session. We suggest that regular consultation sessions be written into the counseling plan. The frequency of such sessions should be determined by the individual nature of each case and the needs that emerge during the counseling process. Such sessions can be very helpful in that they provide an opportunity to obtain complete and specific information about the child outside of sessions.

Principle 8:
Establish the Parameters and Boundaries Necessary to Preserve the Integrity of the Counseling Process

Anchoring the parent or professional to the reality of working with children is also an important part of the consultation process. It is important to be cognizant of the appropriate boundaries that need to be in place and help others understand why these boundaries are important (Mullen, 2008).

Counselors must be prepared to educate parents and professionals who do not understand the foundational principles of working with children;

they must know how child counseling differs from adult counseling. It is critical for counselors working with children to discuss the value and use of art, crafts, games, and play in child counseling interventions. The counseling process is actually a good deal of work for children. But when the element of play (which seems like fun) is added, this can be confusing to parents and professionals. Consider for a moment this statement from a Child Protective Services caseworker:

> *Professional:* I understand that Connor feels more comfortable in a playroom with all the toys and stuffed animals. That should be the time when you need to just ask him to tell you what happens during his visitations with his dad each week. I mean, come on, that is the information we need to know here.

It is essential that counselors make clear to parents and care providers that Child Protective Services should not be setting the counseling agenda. Counseling interventions and treatment plans must remain true to the needs of the child or the agency at the time of referral and adapted appropriately thereafter as treatment progresses. This type of limit setting can be difficult, but an appeal based on the child's best interest can help. One possible response in this type of situation might be as follows:

> *Counselor:* I really appreciate the faith placed in me to elicit the information you need from Connor, but we all might be helped by remembering that our earlier agreement was that Connor's needs must come first. At the current time the counseling plan is based on engaging him in a therapeutic process that does not create space for imposing questions generated from an external source. Thus, I am wondering how we might find an alternative for obtaining the information you need.

Summary

Even counselors who are just beginning their clinical careers know that they cannot convince children to do something that they do not want to do. There is no making a child who enters a counseling office or playroom talk about traumatic events. Behavioral change cannot be forced. Change occurs when the child wants it to. Adults, and even other counselors at times, may believe that they possess some secret or magical power that will make children stop biting, start listening, or start talking about what is bothering them. As any counselor who works with children knows, nothing is further from the truth. Often over the course of counseling change happens, but it happens over time. Moreover, it is as difficult for children as it is for the adults in their lives. Through collaboration and consultation, well-prepared counselors can set the stage so that other stakeholders will have reasonable expectations for both the counselors and the children.

As child counselors work in collaboration and consultation with parents, care providers, and other professionals, they will have many opportunities to provide better services for the children. We believe that collaboration and consultation provide many rich opportunities for all parties involved to grow, change, and learn. Multiple perspectives often result in improved treatments, increased knowledge, and enhanced success for children as they move through their core issues toward a better life (Halstead, 2007).

references

Ablon, S. L. (1996). The therapeutic action of play. *Journal of the American Academy of Child & Adolescent Psychiatry, 35*, 545–548.

American Psychiatric Association. (2000). *Diagnostic and statistical manual of mental disorders* (4th ed., text rev.). Washington, DC: Author.

Antony, M., & Barlow, D. H. (Eds.). (2001). *The handbook of assessment and treatment planning for psychological disorders.* New York, NY: Guilford Press.

Axline, V. M. (1947). *Play therapy* (1st ed.). London, England: Churchill Livingstone.

Axline, V. M. (1969). *Play therapy* (2nd ed.). New York, NY: Ballantine Books.

Babrow, A. S., Kline, K. N., & Rawlins, W. K. (2005). Narrating problems and problematizing narratives: Linking problematic integration and narrative theory in telling stories about our health. In L. M. Hater, P. M. Japp, & C. S. Beck (Eds.), *Narratives, health, and healing: Communication theory, research, and practice* (pp. 31–52). Mahwah, NJ: Erlbaum.

Ball, J., Mitchell, P., & Malhi, G. (2003). Schema-focused cognitive therapy for bipolar disorder: Reducing vulnerability to relapse through attitudinal change. *Australian and New Zealand Journal of Psychiatry, 37*, 41–48.

Barnes, K. L. (2003). Review of: Counseling across the lifespan: Prevention and treatment. *Counselor Education and Supervision, 43*, 78–80.

Beach, S., Wamboldt, M. Z., Kaslow, N. J., Heyman, R. E., & Reiss, D. (2006). Describing relationship problems in *DSM-V*: Toward better guidance for research and clinical practice. *Journal of Family Psychology, 20*, 356–358.

Beck, A. T. (1967). *Depression: Causes and treatment.* Philadelphia: University of Pennsylvania Press.

Beck, A. T., Rush, A. J., Shaw, B. R., & Emery, G. (1979). *Cognitive therapy of depression.* New York, NY: Guilford Press.

Beck, A. T., & Weishaar, M. (1989). Cognitive therapy. In A. Freeman, K. M. Simon, L. E. Beutler, & H. Arkowitz (Eds.), *Comprehensive handbook of cognitive therapy* (pp. 21–36). New York, NY: Plenum.

Beck, A. T., & Young, J. E. (1985). Depression. In D. H. Barlow (Ed.), *Clinical handbook of psychological disorders: A step-by-step treatment manual* (pp. 206–244). New York, NY: Guilford Press.

Boik, B. L., & Goodwin, E. A. (2000). *Sandplay therapy: A step-by-step manual for psychotherapists of diverse orientations.* New York, NY: W. W. Norton.

Burke, J. F. (1989). *Contemporary approaches to psychotherapy and counseling: The self-regulation and maturity model.* Pacific Groves, CA: Brooks/Cole.

Callahan, S., & Panichelli-Mindel, S. (1996). *DSM-IV* and internalizing disorders: Modifications, limitations, and utility. *School Psychology Review, 25,* 297–307.

Cameron, M., & Guterman, N. (2007). Diagnosing conduct problems of children and adolescents in residential treatment. *Child & Youth Care Forum, 36*(1), 1–10.

Cameron, S. (2003). Recognizing the appearance of the self in sandplay therapy. *Journal of Sandplay Therapy, 12,* 133–141.

Campbell, J. (1968). *The hero with a thousand faces.* Princeton, NJ: Princeton University Press.

Carnevale, J. P. (1989). *Counseling gems: Thoughts for the practitioner.* Muncie, IN: Accelerated Development.

Carruthers, C., Hood, C., & Parr, M. (2005). Research update: The power of positive psychology. *Parks and Recreation, 40*(10), 30–37.

Carver, C. S., Scheier, M. F., & Weintraub, J. K. (1989). Assessing coping strategies: A theoretically based approach. *Journal of Personality and Social Psychology, 56,* 267–283.

Cecero, J. J., & Young, J. E. (2001). Case of Silvia: A schema focused approach. *Journal of Psychotherapy Integration, 11,* 217–229.

Chapman, L., Morabito, D., Ladakakos, C., Schrier, H., & Knudson, M. M. (2001). The effectiveness of art therapy intervention in reducing posttraumatic stress disorder (PTSD) symptoms in pediatric trauma patients. *Art Therapy, 18*(2), 100–104.

Chu, J. A. (1992). The therapeutic roller coaster: Dilemmas in the treatment of childhood abuse survivors. *Journal of Psychotherapy Practice and Research, 1,* 351–370.

Comas-Diaz, L. (1996). Cultural considerations in diagnosis. In F. W. Kaslow (Ed.), *Handbook of relational diagnosis and dysfunctional family patterns* (pp. 152–170). New York, NY: Wiley.

Corey, G., Corey, M., & Callanan, P. (2007). *Issues and ethics in the helping professions* (7th ed.). Pacific Grove, CA: Brooks/Cole.

Crawford, E., & Wright, M. (2007). The impact of childhood psychological maltreatment on interpersonal schemas and subsequent experiences of relationship aggression. *Journal of Emotional Abuse, 7*(2), 93–116.

Crenshaw, D. A. (2004). *Engaging resistant children in therapy: Projective drawing and story telling techniques.* Rhinebeck, NY: Revelstoke Community Forest Corporation.

Crenshaw, D. A. (2006). *Evocative strategies in child and adolescent psychotherapy.* Lanham, MD: Rowman & Littlefield.

Cunningham, L. (1997). The therapist's use of self in sandplay: Participation mystique and projective identification. *Journal of Sandplay Therapy, 5*, 121–135.

Cunningham, L. (2003). *Countertransference in sandplay: A symbolic/clinical approach.* Unpublished doctoral dissertation, California Institute of Integral Studies, San Francisco.

De Domenico, G. (1988). *Sand tray world play: A comprehensive guide to the use of sand tray in psychotherapeutic and transformational settings.* Oakland, CA: Vision Quest Images.

De Jong, P. D., & Berg, I. K. (2002). *Interviewing for solutions* (2nd ed.). Pacific Grove, CA: Brooks/Cole.

DiLeo, J. H. (1983). *Interpreting children's drawings.* New York, NY: Brunner/Mazel.

Erickson, F. (2002). Culture and human development. *Human Development, 45*, 299–306.

Erikson, E. (1963). *Childhood and society.* New York, NY: W. W. Norton.

Everly, G. S., & Lating, J. M. (2004). *Personality-guided therapy for posttraumatic stress disorder.* Washington, DC: American Psychological Association.

Flanagan, C. M. (1993). Treating neurotic problems that do not respond to psychodynamic therapies. *Hospital and Community Psychiatry, 44*, 824–826.

Freeman, A. (1993). A psychosocial approach for conceptualizing schematic development for cognitive therapy. In K. T. Kuehlwein & H. Rosen (Eds.), *Cognitive therapies in action: Evolving innovative practice* (pp. 54–87). San Francisco, CA: Jossey-Bass.

Friedman, H. S., & Mitchell, R. R. (Eds.). (2008). *Supervision of sandplay therapy.* New York, NY: Routledge.

Gardner, H. (1980). *Artful scribbles: The significance of children's drawings.* New York, NY: Basic Books.

Gardner, R. A. (1992). *The psychotherapeutic techniques of Richard A. Gardner.* Cresskill, NJ: Creative Therapeutics.

Ginott, H. G. (1961). *Group psychotherapy with children: The theory and practice of play-therapy.* New York, NY: McGraw-Hill.

Gladding, S. T. (2011). *The creative arts in counseling* (4th ed.). Alexandria, VA: American Counseling Association.

Gladstone, A. (1955). Threats and response to threats. *Bulletin of the Research Exchange on the Prevention of War, 3*, 23–31.

Goldfried, M. (2003). Cognitive-behavioral therapy: Reflections on the evolution of a therapeutic orientation. *Cognitive Therapy and Research, 27*, 53–69.

Greenfield, P., Keller, H., Fuligni, A., & Maynard, A. (2003). Cultural pathways through universal development. *Annual Review of Psychology, 54*, 461–490.

Grossmann, K. E., Grossmann, K., & Keppler, A. (2005). Universal and culture-specific aspects of human behavior: The case of attachment. In W. Friedlmeier & P. Hagood (Eds.), *The use of art in counselling child and adult survivors of sexual abuse* (pp. 75–97). London, England: Jessica Kingsley.

Hagood, M. M. (2002). A correlational study of art-based measures of cognitive development: Clinical and research implications for art therapists working with children. *Art Therapy, 19*(2), 63–68.

Halliday, M. A. (1989). *Spoken and written language.* Oxford, England: Oxford University Press.

Halstead, R. W. (1996). The assessment and treatment of relationship wounds. In *The Hatherleigh guide to issues in modern therapy* (pp. 177–200). New York, NY: Hatherleigh Press.

Halstead, R. (2007). *Assessment of client core issues.* Alexandria, VA: American Counseling Association.

Hardy, B. (1977). Narrative as a primary act of the mind. In M. Meek, A. Warlow, & G. Barton (Eds.), *The cool web* (pp. 12–23). London, England: Bodley Head.

Heath, M. A., Sheen, D., Leavy, D., Young, E., & Money, K. (2005). Bibliotherapy: A resource to facilitate emotional healing and growth. *School Psychology International, 26,* 563–580.

Herman, J. (1992). *Trauma and recovery.* New York, NY: Basic Books.

Hoffart, A., Versland, S., & Sexton, H. (2002). Self-understanding, empathy, guided discovery, and schema belief in schema-focused cognitive therapy of personality problems: A process-outcome study. *Cognitive Therapy and Research, 26,* 199–212.

Homeyer, L. E., & Sweeney, D. S. (1998). *Sandtray: A practical manual.* Canyon Lake, TX: Lindan Press.

Homeyer, L. E., & Sweeney, D. S. (2005). Sandtray therapy. In C. A. Malchiodi (Ed.), *Expressive therapies* (pp. 162–182). New York, NY: Guilford Press.

Horvath, A. O., & Greenberg, L. S. (1987). The development of the Working Alliance Inventory. In L. S. Greenberg & W. M. Pinsof (Eds.), *The psychotherapeutic research process: A research handbook* (pp. 529–556). New York, NY: Guilford Press.

Howard, G. (1991). Culture tales: A narrative approach to thinking, cross-cultural psychology, and psychotherapy. *American Psychologist, 46,* 187–197.

Hynes, A. M., & Hynes-Berry, M. (1994). *Biblio-poetry therapy: The interactive process: A handbook.* St. Cloud, MN: North Star Press of St. Cloud.

Ibrahim, F., Roysircar-Sodowsky, G., & Ohnishi, H. (2001). Worldview. In J. G. Ponterotto, J. M. Casas, L. A. Suzuki, & C. M. Alexandra (Eds.), *Handbook of multicultural counseling* (pp. 425–456). Thousand Oaks, CA: Sage.

Jasmine-DeVias, A. (1995). Bibliotherapy: Books that can play a role in helping children work through some of the effects of abuse and neglect. *New England Reading Association Journal, 31,* 2–17.

Kalff, D. M. (1980). *Sandplay: A psychotherapeutic approach to the psyche.* Boston, MA: Sigo Press.

Kaslow, F. (1996). History, rationale, and philosophic overview of issues and assumptions of relational diagnosis. In F. W. Kaslow (Ed.), *Handbook of relational diagnosis and dysfunctional family patterns* (pp. 3–18). New York, NY: Wiley.

Kauffman, J. M. (2001). *Characteristics of emotional and behavioral disorders of children and youth* (7th ed.). Upper Saddle River, NJ: Prentice Hall.

Kegan, R. (1982). *The evolving self.* Cambridge, MA: Harvard University Press.

Kihlstrom, J. (2002). To honor Kraepelin: From symptoms to pathology in the diagnosis of mental illness. In L. Beutler & M. Malkik (Eds.), *Rethinking the* DSM: *A psychological perspective* (pp. 279–303). Washington, DC: American Psychological Association.

Killough-McGuire, D., & McGuire, D. E. (2001). *Linking parents to play therapy: A practical guide with applications, interventions and case studies.* New York, NY: Taylor & Francis.

Kottman, T. (1999). Integrating the crucial Cs into Adlerian play therapy. *Journal of Individual Psychology, 55,* 288–298.

Kottman, T. (2003). *Partners in play: An Adlerian approach to play therapy* (2nd ed.). Alexandria, VA: American Counseling Association.

Kramer, E. (1979). *Childhood and art therapy.* New York, NY: Schocken.

Kramer, E., & Schehr, J. (1983). An art therapy evaluation session for children. *American Journal of Art Therapy, 23,* 3–12.

Landreth, G. (1991). *Play therapy: The art of the relationship* (1st ed.). Muncie, IN: Accelerated Development.

Landreth, G. L. (2002a). *Play therapy: The art of the relationship* (2nd ed.). New York, NY: Brunner-Routledge.

Landreth, G. (2002b). Therapeutic limit setting in the play therapy relationship. *Professional Psychology: Research and Practice, 33,* 529–535.

Langdridge, D. (2005). The child's relations with others. *Journal of the Society for Existential Analysis, 16,* 87–99.

Lazarus, R. S. (1991). *Emotion and adaptation.* New York, NY: Oxford University Press.

Lazarus, R. S., & Folkman, S. (1984). *Stress, appraisal, and coping.* New York, NY: Springer.

Lee, C. W., Taylor, G., & Dunn, J. (1999). Factor structure of the Schema Questionnaire in a large clinical sample. *Cognitive Therapy and Research, 23,* 441–451.

Levi-Strauss, C. (1979). *Myth and meaning.* New York, NY: Schocken Books.

Levitt, J. T., Hoffman, E. C., Grisham, J. R., & Barlow, D. H. (2001). Empirically supported treatments for panic disorder. *Psychiatric Annals, 3,* 478–487.

Lowenfeld, M. B. (1946). Discussion of the value of play therapy in child psychiatry. *Proceedings of the Royal Society of Medicine, 39,* 439–442.

Lowenfeld, M. (1950). The nature and use of the Lowenfeld world technique in work with children and adults. *Journal of Psychology, 30,* 325–331.

Lowenfeld, M. (1960). The world technique. *Topical Problems in Psychotherapy, 3,* 248–263.

Lowenfeld, M. (1993). *Understanding children's sandplay: Lowenfeld's world technique.* London, England: Antony Rowe.

Madden, R. G. (1998). *Legal issues in social work, counseling, and mental health: Guidelines for clinical practice in psychotherapy.* Thousand Oaks, CA: Sage.

Malchiodi, C. A. (Ed.). (1999). *Medical art therapy with children.* London, England: Jessica Kingsley.

Malchiodi, C. A. (Ed.). (2003). *Handbook of art therapy.* New York, NY: Guilford Press.

Malchiodi, C. A. (2005). *Expressive therapies.* New York, NY: Guilford Press.

Malchiodi, C. A. (2006). *Art therapy sourcebook* (2nd ed.). New York, NY: McGraw-Hill.

Malchiodi, C. A. (2008). *Creative interventions with traumatized children.* London, England: Jessica Kingsley.

Maslow, A. (1971). *The farther reaches of human nature.* New York, NY: Harmondsworth.

May, R. (1991). *The cry for myth.* New York, NY: Norton.

Mazza, N. (2003). *Poetry therapy: Theory and practice.* New York, NY: Brunner-Routledge.

McHale, B. (1992). *Constructing postmodernism.* London, England: Routledge.

Morrison, N. (2000). Schema-focused cognitive therapy for complex long-standing problems: A single case study. *Behavioral and Cognitive Therapy, 28,* 269–283.

Moustakas, C. E. (1953). *Children in play therapy: A key to understanding normal and disturbed emotions.* New York, NY: McGraw-Hill.

Muldoon, O. (2003). Perceptions of stressful life events in northern Irish school children: A longitudinal study. *Journal of Child Psychology & Psychiatry & Allied Disciplines, 44,* 193–201.

Mullen, J. A. (2003). Speaking of children: A study of how play therapists make meaning of children. *Dissertation Abstracts International, 64,* 11A.

Mullen, J. A. (2007). *Play therapy basic training: A guide to learning and living the child-centered play therapy philosophy.* Oswego, NY: Integrative Counseling Services.

Mullen, J. A. (2008). *How play therapists can engage parents and professionals.* Oswego, NY: Integrative Counseling Services.

Noble, K. (1994). *The sound of a silver horn: Reclaiming the heroism in contemporary women's lives.* New York, NY: Fawcett Columbine.

Nussbaum, M. C. (1988). Narrative emotion: Beckett's genealogy of love. In S. Hauerwas & L. G. Jones (Eds.), *Why narrative? Readings in narrative theology* (pp. 225–254). Grand Rapids, MI: William B. Eerdmans.

Oaklander, V. (1988). *Windows of our children.* Highland, NY: Gestalt Journal Press.

O'Connor, K. J. (2000). *The play therapy primer.* New York, NY: Wiley.

Orton, R. E. (1996). Discourse communities of teachers and therapeutic philosophy: A response to Douglas Roberts. *Curriculum Inquiry, 26,* 433–439.

Pardeck, J. T. (1994). Using literature to help adolescents cope with problems. *Adolescence, 29,* 421–427.

Pardeck, J. T. (1998). *Using books in clinical social work practice: A guide to bibliotherapy.* New York, NY: Haworth Press.

Pardeck, J. T. (2005). Using bibliotherapy in family health social work practice with children of divorce. In F. K. O. Yuen (Ed.), *Social work practice with youngsters and families: A family health approach* (pp. 45–56). Binghamton, NY: Haworth Press.

Pardeck, J. T., & Pardeck, J. A. (1984). Bibliotherapy: An approach to helping young people with problems. *Journal of Group Psychotherapy, Psychodrama, & Sociometry, 37,* 41–43.

Pardeck, J. T., & Pardeck, J. A. (1993). *Bibliotherapy: A clinical approach for helping children* (Vol. 16). Langhorne, PA: Gordon and Breach.

Pardeck, J. T., & Pardeck, J. A. (1998). An exploration of the uses of children's books as an approach for enhancing cultural diversity. *Early Child Development and Care, 147,* 25–31.

Parry, A., & Doan, R. (1994). *Story re-visions: Narrative therapy in the postmodern world.* New York, NY: Guilford Press.

Pedersen, P. B. (2001). Mobilizing the generic potential of culture-centered counseling. *International Journal for the Advancement of Counseling, 23,* 165–177.

Pedersen, P. B., & Ivey, A. (1993). *Culture-centered counseling and interviewing skills.* Westfield, CT: Praeger.

Pehrsson, D. E. (2006). Fictive bibliotherapy and therapeutic storytelling with children who hurt. *Journal of Creativity in Mental Health, 1,* 273–286.

Pehrsson, D. E. (2007). Co-story-ing: Collaborative story writing for children who fear. *Journal of Creativity in Mental Health, 2*(1), 85–91.

Pehrsson, D.-E., & Aguilera, M. E. (2007). *Play therapy: Overview and implications for counselors.* Alexandria, VA: American Counseling Association.

Pehrsson, D. E., Allen, V. B., Folger, W. A., McMillen, P. S., & Lowe, I. (2007). Bibliotherapy with preadolescents experiencing divorce. *The Family Journal, 15,* 409–414.

Pehrsson, D.-E., & Hoskins, W. J. (Eds.). (2009). *The playbook: Play therapy basics for child-centered counseling.* Las Vegas, NV: Stone Castle Press.

Pehrsson, D. E., & Hoskins, W. J. (2010). *Play therapy basics for child centered counseling.* Las Vegas, NV: Stone Castle Press.

Pehrsson, D. E., & McMillen, P. (2005). Bibliotherapy evaluation tool: Grounding counseling students in the therapeutic use of literature. *Arts in Psychotherapy, 32,* 47–59.

Pehrsson, D. E., & McMillen, P. (2009, March). *Bibliotherapy practices of professional counselors: A national study.* Paper presented at the American Counseling Association Conference and Exposition, Charlotte, NC.

Pehrsson, D. E., & Pehrsson, R. S. (2006). Bibliotherapy practices with children: Cautions for school counselors. *Journal of Poetry Therapy, 19,* 185–193.

Pehrsson, D.-E., & Pehrsson, R. S. (2007). Language fantasy approach: A therapeutic group intervention by creating myths with children. *Journal of Poetry Therapy, 20*(1), 41–49.

Perry, W. (1970). *Forms of intellectual and ethical development in the college years: A scheme.* New York, NY: Holt, Rinehart & Winston.

Piaget, J. (1969). *The psychology of the child.* New York, NY: Wiley.

Polkinghorne, D. (1988). *Narrative knowing and the human sciences.* Albany: State University of New York Press.

Preston-Dillon, D. (1999). *Culturally enhanced interpretations of Jungian sand scenes for multicultural participants: Native American and native Hawaiian perspective.* Unpublished doctoral dissertation, Saybrook Graduate School, San Francisco, CA.

Preston-Dillon, D. (2007). *Sand therapy: An introduction* [Audio course]. Clovis, CA: Association for Play Therapy. Available at www.a4pt.org

Ramsay, J. R. (1998). Postmodern cognitive therapy: Cognitions, narratives, and personal meaning-making. *Journal of Cognitive Psychotherapy, 12,* 39–55.

Ricoeur, P. (1984). *Time and narrative.* Chicago, IL: University of Chicago Press.

Riso, L., du Toit, P., Stein, D., & Young, J. (2007). *Cognitive schemas and core beliefs in psychological problems: A scientist-practitioner guide.* Washington, DC: American Psychological Association.

Rogers, C. (1951). *Client-centered therapy: Its current practice, implications and theory.* London, England: Constable.

Rogers, C. (1961). *On becoming a person: A therapist's view of psychotherapy.* London, England: Constable.

Rubin, J. (1984). *Child art therapy.* New York, NY: Van Nostrand Reinhold.

Rubin, S. G. (2000). *Fireflies in the dark*: The story of Friedl Dicker-Brandeis and the children of Terezin. New York, NY: Holiday House.

Rudolph, C. L., & Thompson, L. B. (2000). *Counseling children.* Pacific Grove, CA: Brooks/Cole.

Schmidt, N. B., Joiner, T. E., Young, J. E., & Telch, M. J. (1995). The Schema Questionnaire: Investigation of psychometric properties and the hierarchical structure of a measure of maladaptive schemas. *Cognitive Therapy and Research, 19,* 295–321.

Schneiders, J., Nicolson, N., Feron, F., Berkhof, J., van Os, J., & deVries, M. (2006). Mood reactivity to daily negative events in early adolescence: Relationship to risk for psychopathology. *Developmental Psychology, 42,* 543–554.

Seligman, L. (1998). *Selecting effective treatments: A comprehensive systematic guide to treating mental disorders.* San Francisco, CA: Jossey-Bass.

Seligman, M. E. (1975). *Helplessness: On depression, development, and death.* Oxford, England: W. H. Freeman.

Seligman, M. E., & Csikszentmihalyi, M. (2000). Positive psychology: An introduction. *American Psychologist, 55,* 5–14.

Sharf, R. S. (2004). *Theories of psychotherapy and counseling: Concepts and cases* (3rd ed.). Pacific Grove, CA: Brooks/Cole.

Shrodes, C. (1950). *Bibliotherapy: A theoretical and clinical-experimental study.* Unpublished doctoral dissertation, University of California at Berkeley.

Sommers-Flanagan, J. (2007). Single-session consultations for parents: A preliminary investigation. *The Family Journal 15*(1), 24–29.

Sommers-Flanagan, J., & Sommers-Flanagan, R. (2004). *Counseling and psychotherapy theories in context and practice: Skills, strategies, and techniques.* New York, NY: Wiley.

Spence, D. P. (2003). Listening for rhetorical truth. *Psychoanalytical Quarterly, 74*, 875–903.

Staub, E. (1999). The roots of evil: Social conditions, culture, personality, and basic human needs. *Personality and Social Psychology Review, 3*, 179–192.

Sterba, S., Egger, H., & Angold, A. (2007). Diagnostic specificity and non-specificity in the dimensions of preschool psychopathology. *Journal of Child Psychology & Psychiatry, 48*, 1005–1013.

Sue, D. W., & Sue, D. (2003). *Counseling the culturally diverse: Theory and practice* (4th ed.). New York, NY: Wiley.

Theiler, S., & Bates, G. (2007). The advantage of accessing early maladaptive schemas in early childhood memories and empirical evidence of their predictive worth. In D. A. Einstein (Ed.), *Innovations and advances in cognitive behaviour therapy* (pp. 267–277). Bowen Hills, Australia: Australian Academic Press.

Todd, R., Huang, H., & Henderson, C. (2008). Poor utility of the age of onset criterion for *DSM-IV* attention deficit/hyperactivity disorder: Recommendations for *DSM-V* and ICD-11. *Journal of Child Psychology & Psychiatry, 49*, 942–949.

Turner, B. A. (Ed.). (2004). *H. G. Wells floor games: A father's account of play and its legacy of healing.* Cloverdale, CA: Temenos Press.

Turner, B. A. (2005). *The handbook of sandplay therapy.* Cloverdale, CA: Temenos Press.

Tursi, M., & Cochran, J. (2006). Cognitive-behavioral tasks accomplished in a person-centered relational framework. *Journal of Counseling & Development, 84*, 387–396.

Vuchinich, S., Angelelli, J., & Gatherum, A. (1996). Context and development in family problem solving with preadolescent children. *Child Development, 67*, 1276–1288.

Wadeson, H. (1980). *Art psychotherapy.* New York, NY: Wiley.

Wadsworth, B. J. (1971). *Piaget's theory of cognitive development.* New York, NY: David McKay.

Wanner, S. (1994). *On with the story: Adolescents learning through narrative.* Plymouth, NH: Boynton/Cook.

White, M. (1986). Negative explanation, restraint, and double description: A template for family therapy. *Family Process, 25*, 169–184.

Witherell, C., & Noddings, N. (Eds.). (1991). *Stories lives tell: Narrative and dialog in education.* New York, NY: Teachers College Press.

Wrosch, C., Scheier, M. F., Carver, C. S., & Schulz, R. (2003). The importance of goal disengagement in adaptive self-regulation: When giving up is beneficial. *Self & Identity, 2*, 1–20.

Young, J. E. (1990). *Cognitive therapy for personality disorders: A schema-focused approach.* Sarasota, FL: Professional Resource Press.

Young, J. E. (1999). *Cognitive therapy for personality disorders: A schema-focused approach* (2nd ed.). Sarasota, FL: Professional Resource Press.

Young, J. E., Beck, A. T., & Weinberger, A. (1994). Depression. In D. H. Barlow (Ed.), *Clinical handbook of psychological disorders* (2nd ed., pp. 240–277). New York, NY: Guilford Press.

Young, J. E., & Flanagan, C. (1998). Schema-focused therapy for narcissistic patients. In E. F Ronningstam (Ed.), *Disorders of narcissism: Diagnostic, clinical, and empirical implications* (pp. 239–262). Washington, DC: American Psychiatric Association.

Young, J. E., & Gluhoski, V. (1997). A schema-focused perspective on satisfaction in close relationships. In R. Sternberg & M. Hojjat (Eds.), *Satisfaction in close relationships* (pp. 356–381). New York, NY: Guilford Press.

Young, J. E., Klosko, J. S., & Weishaar, M. E. (2003). *Schema therapy: A practitioner's guide.* New York, NY: Guilford Press.

Young, J. E., & Mattila, D. (2002). Schema focused therapy for depression. In M. A. Reinecke & M. R. Davison (Eds.), *Comparative treatments of depression* (pp. 292–316). New York, NY: Springer.

Young, J. E., Weinberger, A., & Beck, A. T. (2001). Depression. In D. H. Barlow (Ed.), *Clinical handbook of psychological disorders* (3rd ed., pp. 264–308). New York, NY: Guilford Press.

Zuckerman, M., & Gagne, M. (2003). The COPE revised: Proposing a 5-factor model of coping strategies. *Journal of Research in Personality Assessment, 37,* 169–204.

index

Figures and tables are indicated by f and t following page numbers.

Index